UPPER MISSISSIPPI
A Wilderness Saga

Books *by* Walter Havighurst

Rivers of America books already published are:

THE
RIVERS OF AMERICA

Edited by

STEPHEN VINCENT BENÉT
and CARL CARMER

As Planned and Started by

CONSTANCE LINDSAY SKINNER

Art Editor

RUTH E. ANDERSON

UPPER MISSISSIPPI

A Wilderness Saga

by

WALTER HAVIGHURST

Illustrated by

DAVID AND LOLITA GRANAHAN

FARRAR & RINEHART
INCORPORATED

New York   *Toronto*

This book has been produced in accordance with paper conservation orders of the War Production Board.

TO
JAMES PUTNAM

AUTHOR'S NOTE

Ten years ago, when the Rivers of America was only a project, Constance Lindsay Skinner began to exchange ideas with me about the treatment of the Upper Mississippi. We came to feel that the essential characteristic of the region was the Scandinavian settlement which in the second half of the last century spread from Lake Michigan to the Dakota plains. That folk story, along with an account of the lumbering industry on the Upper Mississippi, became the theme of the book.

Since then, twenty-four volumes of the Rivers of America have appeared. Inevitably in so extended a series the geographical boundaries of individual volumes have been restricted and the narratives have adhered closely to the rivers themselves. To make this volume fit the shape of the series as it has evolved, the present revision has been made. In it the river becomes the principal subject. New themes of river commerce, river settlement, and life on and beside the Mississippi currents replace the folk story of a frontier that moved westward across the great valley. In this revision nothing has been included that does not touch the river or come to it by its tributaries.

Contents

PART FOUR: THE RIVER TODAY

PART ONE

Father of Waters

The sloop "RESTAURATIONEN"
First Emigrant boat — Norway
to the United States — 1825

Canada

WEST · EAST

Lake Superior

NORTH DAKOTA

BISMARCK

TARGO GLYNDON

BEMIDJI LAKE
Source of the Mississippi

DULUTH

CLOQUET

BRAINERD

BRECKENRIDGE

MORRIS

BENSON

MINNEAPOLIS
STILLWATER
ST. PAUL

SOUTH DAKOTA

PIERRE

SIOUX FALLS

MINNESOTA

MINNESOTA RIVER

ST. CROIX

CHIPPEWA FALLS
EAU CLAIRE

WISCONSIN

RHINELANDER

MENOMINEE RIVER
FLORENCE
MENOMINEE
PESHTIGO

WAUSAU

OSHKOSH

MILWAUKEE

Lake Michigan

MICH.

LA CROSSE

WISCONSIN RIVER

MADISON
KOSHKONONG

DUBUQUE

FIRST NORWEGIAN CHURCH
IN AMERICA · Racine Co. Wis.

IOWA

ILLINOIS

CHICAGO

NEBRASKA

MISSOURI RIVER

PLATTE R.

BISHOP HILL

SPRINGFIELD

INDIANA

KANSAS

ST. JOSEPH

MISSOURI

HANNIBAL
SALT R.

KANSAS CITY

ST. LOUIS

CAIRO

Ohio River

The MISSISSIPPI RIVER

The VALLEY
of the
UPPER
MISSISSIPPI

GEORGE
ANNAND

CHAPTER I

Father of Waters

THE Chippewas called their river Mee-zee-see-bee, Father of Waters. Like many of their phrases, this is strong poetry, and though they are a dwindling and almost forgotten people, the name still carries the spell that a great river cast upon the mind of a primitive race. To them the river was one of the lordly and living features of the earth. It was a boundary, a landmark, a highway, a path of light and movement through their ancestral wilderness.

Time has brought many changes since the Chippewa canoes made up the river's commerce, but the Mississippi is still one of the grand and solemn features of America. It has the leisure of everlasting things, it has silence, it has a certainty that makes men feel small and transient as they bridge its currents and launch their commerce from its shores. It was here before history began, and its waters will still make their long, beautiful journey to the sea after the last page of history is recorded.

The Chippewas had never found the river's source —they had neither the curiosity of geographers nor the instruments that could establish the height of land in that bewildering region of lakes, streams, and forests out of which the Mississippi grows. And they had no knowledge of its mouth—the southward-flowing waters were still more than a thousand miles from the sea when they left the domain and the geography of the northern tribes. But they felt the mood of the river and they gave it a majestic name.

The Mississippi, as later explorers ascertained, rises in a high, densely timbered country, near the geographical center of the North American continent. Here, in northern Minnesota, is a watershed that drains into four directions: the headwaters of the St. Lawrence, of Hudson Bay, and of the Mississippi spring from that land of lakes and forests which was the ancestral ground of the Chippewas. The Mississippi's source, long the goal of explorers and geographers, has been located, since its discovery by Henry Schoolcraft in 1832, at Lake Itasca; and that region, with its intricate system of glacial lakes and streams, its splendid groves of pine, its swamps of tamarack, and its swales of wild celery and wild rice, has been fittingly preserved as a State Park. Actually the contour maps now show that Little Elk Lake, five miles above Lake Itasca and 2,466 miles from the Gulf of Mexico, is the ultimate source of the Mississippi.

Little Elk Lake, half a mile long and an eighth of a mile wide, empties into Lake Itasca through Elk, or Excelsior, Creek, and this faint stream is the first flowing of the Father of Waters. Four inches deep and two steps across on the glacial boulders in its bed, the little creek flashes through the water grass and curves under the birch-barred hillside where a few Chippewas live, by seasons, in their wigwams. It moves secretly through weedy swales and grows with the springs that flow down hidden in cattails. Here many travelers find it, and in sport they leap from one reedy bank to the other. Then

they have their boast, to tell in the towns where the
Mississippi is a mile-wide flood, to repeat where
Mississippi is a synonym for grandeur: "Why, I've
stepped across the river. It's a fact, I've straddled the
Mississippi!"

Lake Itasca, 1,470 feet above the sea level, is a
bright and beautiful body of water, seven miles in extent. It is shaped like a Y, with two arms cupped in
the hilly forest of its shores. Beavers still gnaw the
saplings at its edge, deer come down to drink in the late
afternoon, eagles circle to a nest in a tall pine at the
water's rim. The lake has a single island, upon which
Schoolcraft's party landed and made their camp more
than a century ago. It has remained Schoolcraft Island
to this day.

As it flows from the north end of Lake Itasca, the
Mississippi has grown. A man can no longer straddle the
river, though he could wade across it in a few quick
strides. Through forest and swampland it takes its
leisurely and indeterminate way, as though it had no
business with history and the development of a nation.
Bridges straddle it with a pair of ten-foot stringers.
Blackbirds and meadow larks sway on its reeds. Care-
lessly, sometimes brawling over stones and sometimes
lingering through a grassy swale, winding twenty miles
to gain two miles of seaway, it sets out for the distant
Gulf.

In fact, the Mississippi begins to flow northward;
for sixty miles its course moves exactly toward Hudson
Bay. At Lake Bemidji, a flashing expanse of water
rimmed in wooded hills, the river reaches its northernmost point. Out of the east side of Lake Bemidji it flows,

slightly larger now, its course due west, as though destined to flow into Lake Superior. Two more northern
lakes lie in its course—Cass Lake and Winnibigoshish,
large, irregular bodies of water framed in the northern
forest. Beyond Winnibigoshish the river begins to bend
southward through cutover timberlands. It narrows in
stretches of rock-framed channel and again it widens in
swamps where the Indians still harvest the wild rice in
their traditional way, bending the grassy stems over the
gunwales of their canoes, flailing the heads and collecting
the unhulled grains in the vessel's bottom. Wild rice has
long been a delicacy on the Upper Mississippi, and from
those Indian harvests it has found its way to city markets
down the river.

At Brainard the river flows in a deep rock gorge,
and a few miles below that busy county seat town the
Crow Wing River enters from the west, nearly doubling
the Mississippi's size. The enlarged river hurries over a
series of falls and rapids, as evidenced by the towns of
Little Falls and Sauk Rapids, culminating in the Falls
of St. Anthony under the scattered sky line of Minneapolis. There, with the Falls and their attendant rapids,
the river drops eighty feet within a flow of barely half
a mile.

The Twin Cities do not face each other across the
Mississippi, as many travelers mistakenly expect to find
them. The river flows first through Minneapolis and
then curves north again, looping through the city of
St. Paul. So both cities are built on both banks of the
river. A few miles farther south, opposite the town of
Hastings, the St. Croix River adds its tribute to the
Mississippi, and here the river touches its second state,

Wisconsin. Below La Crescent, on its western bank, the
Minnesota shore gives way to Iowa. At this point the
Mississippi has already flowed 1,200 miles. So circuitous
are its headwaters, so many miles does it wander in dark
forests before it swings southward toward the Gulf, that
the river has run one-third of its entire course before it
leaves the state of its origin.

Below the Falls of St. Anthony the Mississippi
channel lies between sandstone bluffs which frame it
grandly for a thousand miles. In that nobly marked
valley the river broadens and narrows, flowing against
one bluff or the other, sometimes filling the whole valley.
Such a broadening occurs at Lake Pepin, a famed and
beautiful section of the Mississippi seventy-seven miles
below St. Paul, where for twenty-five miles the river
fills the entire three-mile space between the lifting
shores. There are legend-haunted heights above the curving river—Maiden Rock, Trempeleau Mountain, Sugar
Loaf, Eagle Bluff, Indian Rock, Diamond Bluff, and
Grandad Bluff. Near Alma, Wisconsin, is a weathered
headland resembling the Great Sphinx of Egypt, and
on the Iowa shore is Pikes Peak, named for Zebulon M.
Pike before he left his name on the map of Colorado.

Above St. Paul the river is dominated by wilderness; though most of the forest has been cut there are
great areas of second-growth timber and whole regions
where the land is still elemental and lonely. From St.
Paul to St. Louis it drains a different country—a fertile
prairie as large as all of France, busy and populous, with
cities spaced along its bluffs. And it is a country rich
in history. Marquette and Jolliet, Father Hennepin and
Julien Dubuque, Peter Pond and Jonathan Carver passed

this way. It is the Mississippi of Chief Black Hawk, making his last stand in the Bad Axe bottoms, of U. S. Grant, stacking hides in his father's tanyard at Galena, of Joseph Smith, leading his harried Mormons to a brief sanctuary at Nauvoo, and of Brigham Young, leading them away on the long trek to Utah; it is the Mississippi of Mark Twain, who first felt the spell of the river sweeping under the bluffs of Hannibal. In the hectic years of the steamboat trade, immigrants thronged the rails, staring at the shores of the new commonwealths that held their future, and fashionable travelers watched the unfolding of the great valley.

The corollary of island is usually lake, or ocean, but the Mississippi is a big river and it contains many islands in its course. In the 660 miles between St. Paul and St. Louis there are more than five hundred islands, not mere bars and ledges but actual islands, large enough to have an individual name, or at least a number. Some of them rise in the midst of the stream, oval in shape, two to three miles in length and covered with a dense growth of cottonwood, maple, and oak forest. A few of the larger islands have been cleared and their fertile, deeply silted acres produce the richest harvest of a rich prairie region. Smaller islands, sometimes bordered with lotus beds, appear in chains, generally close to the river's bank. They are matted with willow thickets, the lower branches often showing a drift of dead leaves that marks the high water of last April. Now many of the islands are joined to the mainland by wing dams which have caused their channels to fill up with silt. Thus in seasons of low water they are no longer islands but tongues of land thrust into the river's current. They give to the channel an endless variety.

In earlier years, when the northern forests covered all the upper country and the water came down the great valley with a full and steady flow, the islands broke the singleness of channel into curving and intimate waterways, and they offered a nearer shore than the upthrust bluffs against the prairie sky. The Upper Mississippi was always varied and nearly always beautiful, and it inspired the mile-long "panoramas" that were shown to marveling crowds in the eastern cities and across the Atlantic.

It takes many streams to make a river. Out of dark forests the first tributaries flow, the Crow Wing, the Minnesota, the St. Croix, the Chippewa, the Zumbrota, Black River, the Bad Axe, the Wisconsin. Other streams flow down from the prairies, Root River, Rock River, the Iowa, the Des Moines, the Illinois. So under the Missouri palisades the Mississippi is a mile-wide flood, dividing the level sweep of land. The yellow current of the Missouri swings in from the far-distant Rockies, and the clear waters of the Ohio bring the rains that fell in Appalachian valleys. At Cairo, Illinois, the Mississippi carries water from twenty-three states and a province of Canada. It draws the snows from the Big Horns and the Alleghenies into the vast midland valley, until the spring that quenched a Pennsylvania farmer's thirst mingles with the sluice that washed a miner's gravel in Montana. Thus augmented, the Mississippi pours on toward the distant Gulf.

From St. Louis to its headwaters the Upper Mississippi is a river in itself, marking a region that has pro-

vided a significant chapter in the American past. Its
people have been shaped by the forces of a mid-con-
tinent wilderness. Some of them are well-known, and
they have important roles in the story of the river. But
most of them are anonymous folk, whose stories are
not singular or celebrated but whose lives are a part
of the common struggle and hope out of which a new
civilization was erected.

There is a rightness in the native tongue and it
seems inevitable now that the great central river should
bear its ancient Chippewa designation. There were several variants of the Algonquin name. Early explorers
trying to convey an Indian word in European spelling
wrote it in a variety of ways: Mich-a-see-bee, Miss-i-
se-pe, Mee-zee-see-bee, and others. Marquette, the river's
discoverer in its upper reaches, approximated our own
version; he spelled it Missisipi. But savage names were
uncouth to the ears of early travelers, and as they drew
their maps they saw a chance to put the mark of their
own culture on the wilderness. Marquette, seeking to
erect the cross in a savage country, wished to name it the
"Conception River," in honor of the Blessed Virgin.
Jolliet, less concerned with evangelism and more with
politics, called it "Buade River," using Count Frontenac's family name. Later, in accord with Frontenac's
sense of politics and at Frontenac's suggestion, he supplanted that name with "Colbert River," in deference
to the great French minister on whom the fortunes of
many in New France depended. Far to the south, where
they found it flowing out of a continent that they did
not even dimly comprehend, the Spaniards gave it a
religious name, the "Rio del Espiritu Santo." Fortunately

all these imported designations have been forgotten and the native name survived. No name from European theology or colonial politics would fit the river that the Chippewas called "Father of Waters."

CHAPTER 2

The Discoverers

THE Mississippi began as legend. To the French explorers and missionaries came rumors, vague as mythology, of a great river in the West. At first it was a legend without a name; it was only a vast river lying somewhere in the unknown wilderness.

When in September of 1634 Jean Nicolet landed on the shores of Green Bay after his voyage of discovery across Lake Michigan, he journeyed at least part way up the Fox River. There he was told by Winnebago tribesmen that he might find a river, three days distant in the west, which flowed into "the great water." Whether or not that river was the Mississippi will never be known. Already the season was late. Now that he had accomplished his mission, the discovery of land beyond the Straits of Mackinac, Nicolet had no reason to risk being caught by winter in that remote country. So he turned back, with his seven Huron paddlers, toward the Huron villages on Georgian Bay. There he wintered, returning to Quebec to report his discoveries in the spring of 1635.

It was twenty-five years before the great river again appeared in the records of western exploration. The story of Radisson and Groseilliers goes, curiously, to a famous library in England and is interwoven with the name of Samuel Pepys, a gentleman of Charles the Second's London, whose fame has no relation to the Mis-

sissippi. In 1880 there was discovered in the Bodleian
Library at Oxford a sheaf of manuscripts written in
labored English by Pierre Esprit Radisson, and recording
four journeys, between 1652 and 1663, into the little-
known interior of North America. The journals proved
to be full of confusion and inconsistency; it was difficult
to determine where Radisson was narrating his own voyages and where he took up the travels of his colleague
and brother-in-law, Médart Chouart Sieur de Groseilliers, who was the older of the two and the more experienced in the western country. Because of the inconsistency of his dates and the confusion of his chronology,
scholars have concluded that Radisson's journals were
written many years after his travels had ended, in fact
after he had settled down to an eventless life in London
and had learned to write a cramped and uncertain English.

On their second voyage to the west, Radisson and
Groseilliers were free-lancing, having set out with no
license from the French governor. This was a long journey, beyond Sault Ste. Marie to the western shores of
Lake Superior. At the end of the second year they led a
caravan of Indian canoes back to the St. Lawrence, laden
with a fortune in peltry. There, because they had gone
without license, the authorities confiscated their cargo.
The two coureurs de bois shortly deserted to the English,
who were striving to gain a hold on the fur trade in the
Northwest. With their help the British organized the
"Company of Adventurers to Hudson's Bay," which
became the greatest fur-trading corporation in history
and, having almost three centuries of unbroken opera-

tion, is now one of the oldest business concerns in the world.

Radisson made his voyages at an incredibly early age; he was just eighteen when he first tramped the portage paths of the unmapped country. After the epic travels of his youth he married an English wife and lived a quiet life in London, apparently untroubled by the memories of an unclaimed empire beyond the Atlantic.

In London he was a friend and neighbor of Samuel Pepys, an antiquarian and historian of the British Navy, and the author, as the world came to know many years after his death, of one of the most curious and revealing of diaries. His diary, written in cipher and certainly intended for no contemporary eye, Pepys had deposited in the library of Magdalen College, Cambridge. It is possible that, antiquarian that he was, he arranged to have the journals of his friend Radisson go to the Bodleian Library at Oxford, where its safekeeping and its ultimate discovery were almost assured.

At any rate, when the Radisson manuscript came to light historians had a new source for their record of exploration in the Upper Mississippi country. The journals were published in 1885 by the Prince Society of Massachusetts, and the fame of Radisson and Groseilliers began.

On the basis of Radisson's journals historians have tried, with considerable disagreement, to reconstruct his itineraries. Some of them regard him and his brother-in-law as the actual discoverers of the Upper Mississippi. Others, perhaps more careful in their reconstruction of the travels of the two traders, allow merely that they visited Green Bay shortly before 1660 and went south and west from there by way of the Fox River and the Wisconsin. The moot point is whether it was the Mississippi that Radisson designated as "the great river that divides itself in 2," adding, "it is so called [the forked river] because it has 2 branches, the one toward the West the other toward the South which we believe runs toward Mexico." Beyond doubt Radisson and Groseilliers did penetrate the Upper Mississippi country in Wisconsin and again in Minnesota, beyond the head of Lake Superior, and whether or not they saw the Mississippi they were the first men of Europe to enter the country that it drains.

The first mention of the Mississippi by name was recorded by the Jesuit missionary Claude Allouez. Father Allouez went out from the St. Lawrence in 1665, making the long and hazardous journey to Chequamegon Bay on Lake Superior, the most remote of the northwest missions, three weeks' journey from his nearest countryman at Sault Ste. Marie. There, at the edge of the vast cold lake, some wandering Illinois Indians told him of a great river called the "Messipi."

In 1668, Jacques Marquette, then thirty-one years of age, left Three Rivers on the St. Lawrence and was never to see civilization again. His first post in the western country was Sault Ste. Marie, where an Indian village straggled beside the mile-long rapids at the foot of Lake Superior. While serving that mission he enjoyed a visit from a veteran voyageur, Louis Jolliet, whose name was later to become imperishably joined with his own. About the same time, though Marquette could then have had no idea that it was coincidence, he talked with a wandering Shawnee Indian who spoke of "a great river which, coming from the Illinois, discharges its waters into that [the South] Sea." To Marquette, as to all the French mapmakers, the South Sea was the sea that would lead to China, and here was reborn the hope, so stubborn and so false, that a water route would be found through the new continent.

Perhaps Marquette's dream of finding the great river began there, beside the loud rapids of the St. Mary's, where Lake Superior water hurried on its long journey to the Gulf of the St. Lawrence. But his next move was to the lonely station at the far end of Lake Superior; he succeeded Allouez at the mission on Chequamegon Bay. There again, this time from roving Illinois tribesmen, he heard accounts of the great river that took its way to a southern sea. On the shores of Lake Superior he shared the hunger and cold of the savages, finally making a miserable journey with them across the wilderness peninsula to St. Ignace on the extreme northern edge of Lake Michigan.

Jean Talon, one of the ablest French officials in Canada, returned from France in 1670 with bold plans for exploration of the interior country. His projects included a thorough mapping of the Hudson Bay region, the seeking of a southern water route around America and to the Orient, and, most urgent and practical of all, the discovery of the Mississippi River, the name of which had appeared with increasing frequency in the reports of traders and missionaries. Talon chose a veteran voyageur, Louis Jolliet, the son of a Quebec wagonmaker, to lead an expedition in search of the Mississippi: and Jacques Marquette, then at the mission of St. Ignace,

was named as chaplain of the party. Before the project
was actively under way Talon was summoned back to
France and Louis XIV sent to Canada one of the great
governors in the annals of New France, Louis de Buade,
Count de Frontenac. Frontenac pushed the plans with
vigor.

To Marquette the word of his appointment with
the expedition brought a deep and joyful satisfaction. At
St. Ignace he was patiently devoting himself to his mission, healing Indian babies of simple illnesses, teaching
the catechism to uncomprehending children, winning
the respect and affection of his savage charges even
though they were slow to grasp his doctrines. But he
had a curiosity about the western country and a burning
desire to carry the cross to tribes whom the French had
not yet encountered. A young man, still in his early
thirties, he was well-equipped for his part in the undertaking; he had physical stamina, a remarkable knowledge of Indian languages, and practiced skill as a mapmaker.

Jolliet and his party arrived at St. Ignace in December of 1672. That winter was spent in preparation, and
on May 17th, when spring was in full beauty over the
northern land and waters, Jolliet, Marquette and their
five companions, in two bark canoes, set out across Lake
Michigan, into Green Bay and up the Fox River. The
Winnebago Indians had tried to frighten them from
their undertaking, warning that their way would be
barred by vicious beasts, boiling rapids and unbearable
heat. Actually they traveled in high spirits and with
good fortune. Hospitable Miami tribesmen guided them
through the wild rice shallows as they neared the port-

age, and then carried their canoes across the mile-wide watershed and saw the travelers on their way down the Wisconsin. Now they were on water flowing westward, carrying them toward country no European had ever seen and regions that had remained featureless on all their maps.

Toward the close of day, on June 17, 1763, when the early summer lushness was over the land, they felt the Wisconsin's current changing and they saw, rolling its flood toward an unknown sea, the great river. There was no questioning it, no doubting it, no mistaking it. Its mood was majesty: it had the vastness of a continent in its flow. They dipped their paddles and the canoes thrust forward. "With a joy I cannot express," Marquette wrote in his journal, they entered the Mississippi.

For a thousand miles the two canoes paddled southward in the Mississippi current. Day after day they passed under the steep shores of Iowa and the grassy slopes of Illinois. Their craft swirled in the swift yellow current of the Missouri, and again in the current of the Ohio. At each juncture of strange waters Marquette guessed right; he thought the Missouri River, which he named the Pekitanoui, would lead toward the California Sea, and he judged that the Ohio came from the Shawnee country.

After a month of southward travel, when they were approaching the mouth of the Arkansas River, they turned back, not wishing to risk an encounter with the Spanish in the lower reaches of the river. Their return voyage, tedious and toilsome against the water's flow, was altered to include some new territory. Halfway on their course they left the Mississippi for the Illinois, finding friendly Indians on that river who guided them across the portage to the Chicago River and directed them to Lake Michigan. They arrived at DePere, at the mouth of the Fox River and the head of Green Bay, late in September—four months and some three thousand miles after they had entered the Fox River on their way to the unknown West.

Another early Frenchman who traced new regions of the Upper Mississippi on the groping maps of the time was Daniel de Greysolon, Sieur Dulhut, popularly known as Duluth. A generous, bold and adventurous man, he was admired by all his French colleagues in the wilderness, among whom generally there was an abundance of rancor and jealousy, and he had an uncanny hold on the Indians. A nobleman by birth, he abandoned in his young manhood the brilliant life of the French court, preferring the hardship and peril of a savage country. He set out from Montreal in 1678 with the immediate purpose of conciliating the Hurons and Ottawas, whose warfare had closed Lake Superior to the fur trade, and with the ultimate dream of finding the long-sought route to the western ocean. Both errands involved great risk and certain hardship, but Duluth's party was made up of reckless young coureurs de bois, robust, lighthearted, and ready for whatever fortunes the wilderness routes might hold.

Duluth promptly succeeded in a venture which lesser men would have called foolhardy and impossible. At the head of Lake Superior, near the site of the city that now bears his name, he made peace between the two great tribes of the Northwest, the Sioux and the Chippewas. More than that, he so won the Indians to him

that the Sioux escorted him to their home far up the
Mississippi. At that point, in the Minnesota forests
around Mille Lacs, he supposed that he was no great
distance from the western sea. When he turned back to
Lake Superior, to complete his meetings with the northern tribes, he left three of his men to explore the country
farther west. After councils with the Assiniboin tribesmen, Duluth himself was ready to seek that salt shore.
He journeyed by way of the Brule and St. Croix rivers to
the Mississippi, where he learned that, since his visit
with them a year before, the Sioux had taken captive
three white men. Their rescue became more urgent with
Duluth than his own explorations, and he set out to
overtake the hunting party which had the captives in
custody. A little distance downstream from the mouth
of the St. Croix he found them, and one of the captives
proved to be a man Duluth had met twice before, on
the battlefield of Seneffe and in the compounds of Montreal. This man was Father Hennepin.

Their meeting is one of the dramatic episodes in the
pageant of the Upper Mississippi. They must have made
a strange picture, Duluth in his blanket coat, leggings
of deerskin, crimson cap and sash, and the Recollect friar
in his gray robes standing among the surly Sioux. Now,
in the wilderness, beside the solemn flow of the Mississippi, five thousand miles from the Flanders battlefield
where Duluth had been a fighting man and Hennepin
had knelt on the trampled ground to confess the dying,
they met again.

The year before, 1679, Father Hennepin had journeyed with La Salle's expedition to Green Bay in the
historic *Griffin*, the first sailing vessel on the Lakes,

which La Salle had built above Niagara Falls. While La Salle turned south down the Mississippi, Hennepin and two companions had been sent north to explore the upper reaches of the river. But they had fallen into the hands of the Sioux, and for four months they were taken by their captors from one hunting ground to another. Now, Duluth, in a dramatic demonstration of his power with the Indians, demanded their immediate release.

Despite the restriction of being a captive (an indignity which he later tried to conceal) Father Hennepin had seen a good deal of new country. The Sioux had taken him up the Mississippi and through the forests to Mille Lacs. On their way south Hennepin discovered (for the mapmakers) and named the Falls of St. Anthony, which he later reported as a thundering cataract half as high as Niagara. Neither nature nor Hennepin's own adventures suffered when, back in the gray cities of Europe, he sat down to write the story of his travels in the wilderness.

La Salle, the leader of the expedition which took Hennepin to the West, built Fort Crêvecoeur at Peoria Lake on the Illinois River, leaving his lieutenant, Henry de Tonty, in command while he returned to Fort Frontenac for supplies. Tonty, a cousin, by the relationship of his French mother, of Duluth's, was a resolute man who became famous among the Indians as "the man with the iron hand." In a naval battle off the coast of Spain he had hacked off a maimed hand with his own sword; now he wore on his wrist a hook of metal, and often in the wilderness it served him as an implement and a weapon, impervious alike to frost and fire. His spirit, too, was hardy and indomitable; he survived al-

most incredible hardships before he made his great journey down the Mississippi with La Salle.

After La Salle had left the log stockade on Lake
Peoria his rebellious men during Tonty's absence burned
the fort and fled into the forest. On his return to the
scene of ruin Tonty did what he could to put the place
in order and proceeded to gather furs and strengthen
his friendship with the Indians. Early that autumn, with
La Salle still unaccountably absent, a war party of hos-
tile Iroquois, traditional enemies of the Illinois, appeared
at Fort Crêvecoeur. Tonty was painfully wounded before he succeeded in making peace with the invaders.
When, shortly afterward, the Illinois tribesmen disappeared down the river, Tonty, with six loyal Frenchmen, was left without provisions in a perilous country.
They concluded that they must try to reach the Green
Bay mission, three hundred miles to the north. Accordingly they loaded their goods into a leaky canoe and
started toward the portage that would lead them to the
Chicago River and Lake Michigan. By the time they
reached the lake they were reduced to grubbing the
ground for wild potatoes and wild onions.

At Lake Michigan they repaired their canoe and
pointed it northward. But they were weak, their leader
was still suffering from the wound inflicted by the
Iroquois, and winter was approaching. On All Souls'
Day, November 2nd, the waves of an autumnal storm
wrecked their canoe on the shore above the mouth of the
Milwaukee River. Wandering through the woods, they
became lost in snowstorms; the icy swamps lacerated
their feet and legs. For eleven days they wandered, until
they found an Indian village on the Lake Michigan

shore. The village was deserted, its inhabitants being away in the woods for the witner hunting, but the famished party found shelter and firewood, some fragments of food and a sound canoe on the beach. Gathering a little store of Indian corn and some frozen gourds, they set out again. But other disappointments and hardships awaited them. When one of the men fell ill from eating boiled leather they felt their hope expiring. In that extremity they were found by two friendly Ottawa hunters who helped them to a camp where Indian women thawed their frozen limbs, tended Tonty's wound and brought them back to strength.

It was not until the next summer that Tonty met his chief, La Salle. The meeting occurred at St. Ignace and was a reunion of men who had thought each other dead.

The next year, 1682, they made their memorable voyage down the Mississippi. Starting in midwinter, when they were compelled to use sledges on the frozen Illinois River, they reached the Mississippi in February and floated down the river as spring moved up the great valley. In April they reached the delta, where La Salle planted the royal arms and proclaimed the river and all lands drained by it to be by right of discovery the dominions of Louis XIV, King of France. With that event for the first time in history the great river was traced from its upper tributaries to the Gulf. The Mississippi remained the discovery of De Soto in the south and of Jolliet and Marquette in the north, but to La Salle and Tonty went the honor of bridging those two discoveries and claiming the whole empire of "Louisiana" for France. In the lonely and fruitless years that followed, before La Salle was murdered by his own mutinous men and while Tonty kept remote fur posts among the Indians, that triumphant voyage must have been a heartening memory.

Two hundred and fifty years after Marquette and Jolliet swung their canoes into the Mississippi's current a celebration was held on the site of their discovery. At Prairie du Chien, Wisconsin, above the mouth of the Wisconsin River, ten thousand people gathered on Campion Field to observe the anniversary. After a series of addresses a historical pageant was presented by six hundred people against a background of the bluffs which stand unchanged since the French explorers found the broad river moving between its lifted shores. The celebration closed with the unveiling of a granite memorial on the heights of Nelson Dewey State Park. The unveiling took place in the long June evening, as the western light slanted across the river and touched the bluffs with gold, very close, it was said, to the hour of the explorers' own arrival there. The words in granite will endure like memory, while the river moves on toward the sea. At *the foot of this eminence Jacques Marquette and Louis Jolliet entered the Mississippi River, June 17, 1673.*

CHAPTER 3

Bales of Beaver Skins

IN ITS great years the fur trade appeared to enrich both parties to it. The Indians were puzzled and overjoyed at the eagerness of traders to exchange guns, traps, kettles, blankets, knives and whisky for their worn beaver robes; and the traders ranked those same skins at the top of the six grades of beaver. They called it winter greased beaver: it was beaver captured in the frozen months when the pelt was thickest, and it was greased by the oil of the Indians' own bodies, having been worn by them until the long hairs fell out and the skin was soft and supple. Next in value was the half-greased winter beaver, being newer pelts not so thoroughly worn, and this was followed by greased summer beaver. At the bottom of the list were the pelts which were not taken off the Indian's back, dry winter beaver and dry summer beaver. It was bales of these furs that made the first commerce on the Upper Mississippi, long before the river carried its cargoes of lead from the Wisconsin mines, its log rafts from the northern forests, its harvests of grain from the prairies.

Nicolas Perrot was the founder of the rich trade in peltry on the upper river, and in the course of his undertakings he formed alliances with the Indians which ensured for a century French sovereignty in the western wilderness. He built forts and trading posts on the

Upper Mississippi, discovered the lead mines that eventually supplanted the fur trade in the river's commerce, and took possession of vast territory in the name of France.

All this was the achievement of a small man, whom the Algonquin tribes called Metaminena, "Little Indian Corn," and some historians have regarded as the greatest Frenchman in the West. He began his life in New France in the service of the Jesuits, but when he went to the West in 1668 the zeal for baptizing savages gave way to a zeal for beaver peltry. From his first encounters with the Indians, on the shores of Lake Superior and along the rivers of Wisconsin, he proved to have great influence with them. When he fired his gun, not in threat but in response to a joyous demonstration of Menominee youths, they thought him a deity just dropped down from the sun. He found remote tribes in possession of French knives and hatchets, dulled and broken, having passed from village to village; the French goods had gone to places that the traders had never seen. Everywhere that Perrot went the savages were eager for his trade. They held feasts and dances in his honor. They staged sham battles and conducted contests of lacrosse. They carried him in triumph from one village to another, and at each place they spread robes for him to rest upon and solemnly presented him with the ceremonial pipe. Everywhere they admired the axes, kettles, and knives he had brought for their trade and marveled that anyone should come so far to exchange such wares for their worn-out beaver robes.

In 1670 Perrot returned to the St. Lawrence to report his alliances with the western tribes. Before the season was over he was on his way to the wilderness again, but winter forced him to take shelter with the Amikwa tribesmen on Georgian Bay. Again he proved his power and popularity with the savages. They took him with them on a great hunt on Manitoulin Island, where with primitive snares they slaughtered 2,400 moose. There were feasting and festivity before Little Indian Corn pushed on, with the breaking up of winter's ice, toward the rivers of Wisconsin.

Early that summer he led a delegation of the tribes to Sault Ste. Marie for a great pageant of annexation. On a hill above the St. Mary's rapids, on June 14, 1671, in the presence of missionaries, traders, and numbers of all the northern tribes, possession was declared in the name of "the Most Redoubtable Monarch Louis" to all the countries, rivers, lakes, "those discovered and to be discovered," bounded on one side by the Northern and Western Sea and on the other by the South Sea. This proclamation might seem sufficiently inclusive and final. But because the Indian memory was short and the British continued to assert their right to trade in the West, it was necessary to take possession repeatedly.

Perrot himself did more than any other man to make the claim a reality. In 1685 he built a wintering post beside the Mississippi under Mount Trempeleau, "the mountain that steeps itself in the water," one of the most dramatic sites on the upper river. The next spring he took his men upstream to Lake Pepin and erected Fort St. Antoine, and shortly after built Fort St. Nicolas at Prairie du Chien, where the Wisconsin enters the Father of Waters. These were the earliest establishments erected on the Upper Mississippi.

At Fort St. Antoine, between the bold hills and the wide waters of Lake Pepin, Perrot staged another pageant of possession. On May 8, 1689, with spring's first green on the hills and the Mississippi flowing full, in the company of a few French traders, a black-robed priest, and a host of staring Sioux, Little Indian Corn took claim to all the lands drained by the "Missicipi," as well as of "other places more remote." Over the water went shouts of "Vive le roi!" and the chants of Latin hymns. In the next season canoe caravans laden with baled peltry passed in long processions through the rivers, across the lakes, over the portages and so at last, by the famous Nipissing route, to the tall ships waiting beside the warehouses on the St. Lawrence.

Another Frenchman who was lured from the Jesuit service by the fur trade was Pierre Le Sueur. While serving as an assistant in the mission at Sault Ste. Marie he saw the Indians and the voyageurs coming in from the portage trails and he heard stories of the scattered posts in the Upper Mississippi country. Soon he was trading among the Sioux in the Minnesota forests, and he became so popular with the Indians that the St. Pierre River was named for him. For a hundred years that name appeared on maps of the Northwest before the St. Pierre became the Minnesota River.

In 1689 he was with Perrot on the shores of Lake Pepin. In the next decade he himself built a post near the head of Lake Superior and another on Prairie Island in the Mississippi, just above Lake Pepin. From these points he carried on a profitable trade in peltry and raised the prestige of the French among the savages. As Duluth had done sixteen years earlier, and with no more lasting results, he negotiated a peace between the Sioux and their traditional enemies, the Chippewas, and won the allegiance of both barbarous tribes to France.

When in 1697 he was unable to renew his trading license, Le Sueur went to France and obtained a grant to develop a "valuable" mine whose discovery he had guarded against just such a time as this. He returned to America by way of the Gulf of Mexico instead of the Gulf of St. Lawrence, arriving at the mouth of the Mississippi in the summer of 1700. For his mining enterprise he built a small sailing vessel and assembled a crew of twenty men, and thus ascended the great valley to the river that bore his name. He made his way up that stream to the mouth of the Blue Earth River, where he built a stockade and proceeded to load his craft with two tons of blue-green clay, supposing it to be copper ore. That worthless cargo he floated two thousand miles to Louisiana, with the intent of shipping it to France. He died soon after his arrival at the mouth of the Mississippi, unaware of the futility of his final enterprise.

Despite the boldness of the French traders and the courageous devotion of the missionaries, New France was never an empire, but only the dream of one. The governors on the St. Lawrence visioned a colony embracing the whole domain of the Great Lakes and the valley of the Mississippi, but they had only a few thousand men coming and going through leagues of wilderness. Their possession consisted of scattered posts, sometimes as far apart as the breadth of France, and an occasional bark chapel beside an Indian trail. Such a dream must end, and on an August night in 1759 when General James

Wolfe directed his barges across the dark St. Lawrence the end was at hand. Under cover of darkness the red-coated troops scaled the heights of Quebec. General Wolfe chose his battleground on the Plains of Abraham and waited for the French. When that battle was over the curtain had fallen on the empire of New France. A thousand miles away, beside another river deep in wilderness, over the lonely trading posts the flag of Britain rippled in the wind.

For the next half century the British dominated the fur trade, using the French and half-breed voyageurs but sending their own clerks and factors to administer the stations. Though they made no attempt to occupy the country they mapped the Upper Mississippi valley with great care and planted their garrisons at strategic points throughout the Northwest.

During this period Jonathan Carver made his famous journey up the river. It was not, actually, so famous a journey as he had in mind to make. Though he was a quiet, reflective man, fifty-seven years old when he began his western travels, Carver was bent on an expedition across the continent and the establishing of a fur post on the "Oregon." He was, in fact, hoping to discover the long-desired sea route to the Orient. Though his journey took him no nearer than two thousand miles from the Pacific Ocean, it did result in the first English description of the Upper Mississippi and in the appearance of one of the most famous and most disputed books ever published.

In 1766 Jonathan Carver, a New England shoemaker who had acquired some reputation as a mapmaker, was sought out in Boston by Major Robert

Rogers, the famous Ranger of the French and Indian
War. For eight shillings a day Rogers engaged him to
accompany an expedition to the West and to make "observations, surveys and drafts" of the unexplored country. Rogers was assigned to command the British post at
Michilimackinac; that wilderness station appealed to
him as the springboard to a dream he had harbored for
years, the finding of the fabled Northwest Passage. He
made his plans accordingly.

In September, 1766, under Rogers's orders, Jonathan
Carver left Michilimackinac for Green Bay and the Fox,
Wisconsin and Mississippi rivers. As the first part of his
undertaking he was to map the Mississippi as far north
as the Falls of St. Anthony, and then to await further
orders. Carver carried out his instructions, ascending the
Mississippi to the Falls and wintering in that country
with the Sioux. In the spring, still without new orders
or fresh supplies, he descended the river to the mouth
of the Wisconsin, where he was met by Rogers's agents
with orders to accompany them north to Lake Winnipeg. The party journeyed up the Mississippi and Chippewa rivers, then portaged to the Bois Brule and so entered Lake Superior. When they reached the post of
Grand Portage on the north shore of the lake they found
a letter from Rogers confessing that because of difficulties with his superiors he could not send them the supplies he had agreed to furnish, though he urged them to
continue with their project of exploration. Without supplies or the prospect of them, the party agreed to abandon the expedition and return directly to Mackinac. So
ended, almost before it began, another attempt to find
the Northwest Passage.

In 1768, after two years' absence, Carver was back in New England. He tried in vain to collect from the British military authorities the wages that Rogers had promised him; then he tried without success to publish the journals of his travels. It seemed that his western adventure had treated him shabbily. But the end was not yet. In the hope of interesting an English publisher in his journal he sailed the next year for London, where he remained during the final years of his life. There he made the ill-founded expedition famous and began a controversy that has not ended yet.

In 1778, two years before his death, there was published in London *Travels Throughout the Interior Parts of North America in the Years 1766, 1767, and 1768,* by Jonathan Carver. Within a few years there were twenty-three editions of the book and the name of Jonathan Carver was known in every country of Europe and in America. The *Travels* enjoyed not only a popular success but a critical one as well. Moses Coit Taylor in his authoritative *Literary History of the Revolution* found in it "the charm of a sincere, gentle, powerful personality," as well as "the charm of novel and significant facts, of noble ideas, of humane sentiments," all uttered in a pure and disciplined style.

The success came too late for Carver. He died in dire poverty, just before his book began a long and brilliant life making the Mississippi wilderness and its savage tribes known to readers in many languages. From its pages Chateaubriand drew deeply for his romantic descriptions of Indian life, and the poet Schiller derived the conception and material for his famous "Indian Death-Dirge." Reading the *Travels* in a hill-locked

Massachusetts village young William Cullen Bryant,
brooding on death and the vast American landscape,
shaped the sonorous lines of "Thanatopsis"—

> Or lose thyself in the continuous woods
> Where rolls the Oregon, and hears no sound
> Save his own dashings.

Carver's work became a source-book and a classic for
all who could be interested in interior America.

After a few years, however, the famous book began
to attract question and suspicion. Upon critical exam-
ination it was found to be filled with inaccuracies and
with passages made up in long paraphrase from Charle-
voix's *Journal*, La Hontan's *New Voyages to North
America*, Adair's *History of the North American Indians*, and other authoritative works on North America
—none of which had attained more than a fraction of the
success that came to Carver's suspect *Travels*. The critics
of Carver concluded that his book was the work of some
literary hack of London who used the rough notes in
Carver's journeys and wove into them plagiarized material from other sources. Carver's admirers came to his
defense and did much to restore his book to its former
place as authentic narrative. The controversy is not
ended; but the book remains, however it was produced,
the first English record of travel in the Upper Mississippi country, a classic work whose success could not
mitigate the poverty and disappointment in which Jonathan Carver died.

One product of Carver's fame was the appearance
for many years after his death of "Carver scrip," by
which claimants sought to gain title to some of the most

valuable lands in Minnesota and Wisconsin. Carver had told of witnessing burial procedures above the Mississippi on the site of what is now the Indian Mounds Park in the city of St. Paul. At the same time he entered a cavern under Dayton Bluff and there in a solemn ceremony two Sioux chiefs granted Carver and his heirs a large tract of land along the Mississippi. The cavern, since known as Carver's Cave, became an object of great interest to steamboat visitors to St. Paul and was made famous by the extended litigation over "Carver Scrip." This scrip, based on the supposed grant made by the Sioux chiefs, was sold by speculators who secured it from Carver's heirs. For years hopeful possessors of the scrip came to St. Paul and claimed areas of richly developed property along the Mississippi. The claims went ultimately to the federal Congress where after twenty years of indecision the alleged treaty between Carver and the Indians was annulled.

But Carver's Cave still opens on the banks of the Mississippi. Carver's *Travels* still works upon the minds of historians and artists, and Carver's scrip occasionally turns up at the capitol in St. Paul. So the fruitless journey of a quiet, patient, faintly melancholy man up the wilderness river remains a living story.

Another New Englander who figured prominently on the Upper Mississippi in the years of British domination was Peter Pond. A shrewd and restless Yankee, Peter Pond served with the British in the French and Indian War, after which he took a trading trip to the West Indies. In 1765 he entered the western fur trade, and soon was the boldest and most successful man in the interior country.

For twenty-five years he roved the great Northwest, trading first with the Sioux on the Upper Mississippi and then striking north through wild Canadian wastes to Lake Winnipeg, the Saskatchewan and Lake Athabasca. In the course of his trade he secured rich harvests of peltry and his name was known over a thousand miles of primitive territory. Such success inevitably brought rivalry and opposition. In the lonely Canadian brush he had a quarrel with a Swiss trader named Wadin; Pond shot and killed his rival. The episode was common knowledge in the North, but Pond never stood trial for the trader's death because no court had jurisdiction in that remote place. A few years later, on the bleak shores of Great Slave Lake, he fought a duel with John Ross, a noted Scotch trader; John Ross was buried beside the cold waters of that lonely lake.

In his early seasons in the Saskatchewan country Pond had pooled interests with Alexander Henry and the famous Frobisher brothers. This association resulted in the great North West Company; when that company was formed in 1783 Pond held one of its sixteen shares. In 1788 he left the far-flung posts, sold out his share of North West stock and returned to the order and quiet of Milford, Connecticut.

The later life of Peter Pond was well-known to students of western trade and exploration, but the story of his early enterprise on the Upper Mississippi did not come to light until sixty years after his death. In 1868 at Hartford, Connecticut, a document was found in the kitchen of the governor's mansion. At that time the governor of Connecticut was Charles Hobby Pond, the fur trader's nephew, and the manuscript proved to be

Peter Pond's journal of his first seasons on the Upper Mississippi. It was found in a box of waste paper, only partially complete. An undetermined number of pages had been used to kindle the kitchen fires.

What remained of Peter Pond's journal was printed in the *Connecticut Magazine,* as much for its incredible and fascinating spelling as for its historical value. But it was soon recognized as a valuable account of the western country in a period when there was no English record except Carver's fiercely disputed *Travels.*

Some forty pages of the journal had escaped the kitchen fire. They make up a vivid, sometimes evocative picture of the posts and portage paths, the Indians and traders, the forests and shores of the Upper Mississippi in the years of the American Revolution. Here is a typical fragment:

> After Suplying myself with such Artickels as I wanted and thay Had to Spare I gave them sum creadeat and Desended the River to the Mouth which Empteys into the Massaippey and Cros that River and Incampt. The Land along the River as you descend Appears to be Exalant. Just at Night as we ware InCampt we Perseaved Large fish Cuming on the Sarfes of the Water. I had then a Diferant trader with me who had a number of Men with him. We were Incampt Near Each other. We Put our Hoock and Lines into the Water and Leat them Ly all nite. In the Morning we Perseaved thare was fish at the Hoocks and went to the Wattr Eag and halld on our line. Thay Came Heavey. At Lengh we hald one ashore that wade a Hundered and four Pounds—a Seacond that was One Hun-

dered Wate—a third of Seventy five Pounds. The
Men was Glad to Sea this for thay Had not Eat mete
for Sum Days nor fish for a long time. We asked
our men How meney Men the largest would Give
a Meale. Sum of the Largest Eaters Sade twelve
men Would Eat it at a Meal. We Agread to Give
ye fish if they would find twelve men that would
undertake it. Thay Began to Dres it. The fish was
what was Cald the Cat fish. It Had a large flat Head
Sixteen Inches Betwene the Eise. Thay Skind it—
Cut it up in three larg Coppers Such as we have
for the Youse of our men. After it was Well Boild
thay Sawd it up and all Got Round it. Thay began
and Eat the hole without the least thing with it But
Salt and Sum of them Drank of the Licker it was
Boild in. The Other two was Sarved out to the
Remainder of the People who finished them in Short
time. Thay all Declard they felt the Beater of thare
Meale Nor did I Perseave that Eney of them ware
Sick or Complaind. Next Morning we Recrost ye
River which was about a Mile Brod and Mounted
about three Miles til we Come to the Planes of the
Dogs [Prairie du Chien] so Cald the Grate Plase of
Rondavues for the traders and Indians Before thay
Dispars for thare Wintering Grounds. Hear we
Meat a Larg Number of french and Indians Make-
ing out thare arrangements for the InSewing winter
and sending of thare cannoes to Differant Parts—
Like wise Giveing Creadeats to the Indans who ware
all to Rondovouse thare in Spring. I Stayed ten days
Sending of my men to Different Parts. I had Nine
Clerks which I Imploid in Differant Rivers that fel
into the River.

Pond had a curiosity about the country his trade took him through and a sharp eye for the ways of the Indians. As he penetrated new regions up the Mississippi and Minnesota rivers, his record is that of a quick, fresh, frank observer, realistic and discerning, amid a landscape and a people then unknown to the world.

In Winter the Natives near the Mouth of the [Minnesota] River Rase Plentey of Corn for thare One Concumtion. The Manners and Customs of ye Yantonose—the Band I saw up the River are Nottawases by Nation But by Sum Intarnal Dispute thay ware Separated into Six Differant Bands Each Band Lead by Chefes of thare One Chois. . . . These ware One Nation formaley and Speke the Same Langwege at that Day. Ye Yantonose [Yanktons] are faroshas and Rude in thare Maners Perhaps Oeing in Sum masher to thare Leadig an Obsger life in the Planes. Thay Seldom Sea thare Nighbers. Thay Leade a wandering Life in that Extensive Plane Betwene the Miseura & Missicippey. Thay dwell in Leather tents Cut Sumthing in form of a Spanish Cloke and Spread out by thirteen in the shape of a Bell—the Poles Meet at the top But the Base is forten in Dimerter—thay Go into it By a Hole Cut in the Side and a Skin Hung Befour it By Way of a Dore—thay Bild thare fire in the Middel and do all thare Cookery over it—at Night thay Lie down all around the Lodg with thare feet to the fire. Thay Have a Grate Number of Horses and Dogs which Carres there Bageag when thay Move from Plase to Plase. Thay Make youse of Buffeloes dung for fuel as there is but little or no Wood on the Planes. Thay are Continuely on the

Watch for feare of Beaing Sarprised By thare En-
emies who are all Round them. Thare war Implements are sum fire armes, Boses and arroes & Spear
which thay have Continuely in thare hands. When
on the March at Nite the Keep out Parteas on the
Lookout. Thay Run down the Buffelow with thare
Horses and Kill as Much Meat as thay Please. In
Order to have thare Horseis Long Winded thay Slit
thair Noses up to the Grissel of thair head which
Make them Breath Verey freely. I Have Sean them
Run with those of Natrall Nostrals and Cum in
Apearantley Not the Least Out of Breath. These
when a parson dies among them in winter thay
Carrea the Boddey with them til thay Cum to Sum
Spot of Wood and thay Put it up on a Scaffel till
when the frost is out of the Ground thay Intare it.
Thay Beleve in two Sperits—one Good & one Bad.
. . . Thay Make all thare Close of Differant Skins.
These Parts Produse a Number of Otters which
Keep in Ponds and Riveleats on thee Planes and Sum
Beavers but the Land Anamels are the Mane Object
of the Natives.

The Spring is now advancing fast.

The Chefes Cuming with a Number of Natives
to Go with me to Mackenac to Sea and Hear what
thare farther Had to Say . . .

At this point the manuscript breaks off, the rest
of Peter Pond's narrative having kindled the fire to boil
his nephew's breakfast eggs.

In the early years of American domination Prairie
du Chien became the center of the fur trade on the
Mississippi. Every spring the tribes came down the rivers

to barter their furs for goods shipped from St. Louis on flatboats. The painted Indians stalked among the boatmen and traders, and the highhearted coureurs de bois swaggered through the compounds in their scarlet caps and sashes.

Joseph Rolette, though Canadian born, became a leading figure in the American fur trade and was known as "King Rolette" by voyageurs all over the upper country. A quick, restless man, the Indians called him Zica, "the Pheasant," because he traveled so fast: but he was also a shrewd merchant and the tribes had another name for him Ahkayzaupectah, "Five More," because of his insistence on a good bargain in his trade for their peltry. His trading interests did not rob him of generosity. Wherever he went, among merchants or savages, in the woods or at the settlements, he carried the vivacity and good humor that made him famous. Long after his death men on the Upper Mississippi remembered King Rolette.

While King Rolette was enjoying life at Prairie du Chien, a young clerk named Hercules Dousman was learning the fur trade at its capital on Mackinac Island. In 1826 he was sent to Prairie du Chien to serve as a clerk under Rolette, but Dousman was not designed to serve anyone except himself. King Rolette was a restless, roving man, and Dousman stayed at his desk, learning the business, planning for its future, watching commerce growing on the Mississippi, investing, cautiously at first and then more confidently, in river craft, entrenching himself in the economic life of the Upper Mississippi. Before Rolette died in 1842, Dousman had supplanted him as agent at Prairie du Chien. After Rolette's death, Dousman married his beautiful young widow and built for her the famed Villa Louis on the site of the vanished Fort Crawford. The fur trade was not to last much longer on the Mississippi but it lasted long enough to make Hercules Dousman a powerful and wealthy man. Villa Louis still stands on its commanding ground above the river, furnished as it was a hundred years ago, a showplace and a memorial of the first rich commerce of the Mississippi.

CHAPTER 4

Search for the Headwaters

THE mouth of the Mississippi was known two hundred years before its source was found. The river rises from the highest land between the Alleghenies and the Rocky Mountains, but it is also a dark land, of forest swamps and glacial lakes and a bewildering network of streams gradually finding their way toward the descending valley. Such a country offered many obstacles to an explorer. In winter the waters were locked in ice and an expedition must abandon its boats, hauling its goods on sledges across the frozen swamps and over the stilled, snow-drifted rivers. Then there was no flowing water to lead men to the river's beginning. In summer the water was a movement through the land, but the swamps were impassable and streams were blocked by blowdowns and the sturdy dams of beavers. It was a country further overshadowed by the long and bloody warfare of the Sioux and Chippewa nations. So for generations the Mississippi kept the secret of its birth.

Though the Revolutionary War brought recognition of the claim of the United States to all land east of the Mississippi, in actuality the British continued to control the garrisons and posts of the Northwest. It was not a short or easy task for a young nation to extend control over a vast unorganized territory. Then in 1803 the farsighted President Jefferson negotiated the Louisi-

ana Purchase and the United States obtained an enormous new empire, at a little more than two cents an acre.
The bounds of the nation far outran its authority.

Promptly in 1803 Jefferson ordered Lewis and
Clark to find the headwaters of the Missouri River and
to seek streams beyond the Continental Divide which
would lead to the Pacific. Two years later a young
United States Army officer, Lieutenant Zebulon M. Pike,
was authorized to lead an expedition to the headwaters
of the Mississippi.

Pike was well-equipped for his mission. Besides his
own youth, courage, and resourcefulness, he had at St.
Louis a party of twenty men and a seventy-foot keelboat loaded with provisions and goods for trade with the
Indians. With a favorable wind he could make twenty
miles a day against the river's current.

Now that expedition is regarded as a venture in
exploration. Actually Pike had a threefold mission: he
was to make peace (again) between the Sioux and the
Chippewas, to assert the rights of United States traders
on the upper river, and to map the Mississippi's headwaters. In none of these undertakings was he completely
successful. For sixty gallons of whisky and two hundred
dollars' worth of knives, hatchets, and kettles, he acquired from the Indians military sites where the St.
Croix and the Minnesota rivers join the Mississippi. That
seemed a great bargain, until it was discovered that the
Indians continued their allegiance to the British and
fought for them a few years later in the War of 1812.
Winter overtook Pike when he was just 120 miles north
of St. Anthony's Falls, and still a long, hard way from
the river's source. At that point he built a blockhouse

and stationed part of his men. With snowshoes and sledges the rest of them pushed on. Plodding through the frozen swamps in the bitter winter he reached the icy expanse of Leech Lake on the last day of January, 1806. This was his farthest penetration, and he was still more than a hundred miles, as the river flows, from the source of the Mississippi. Though he raised American flags over the outlying trading posts he had no sooner disappeared on the spring crest of water than the traders hauled down his flags and sent their peltry out to the Canadian stations.

Zebulon Pike returned to St. Louis on the last day of April, 1806. He went on with a brief and eventful career, to fame as an explorer of the Rocky Mountains and to death in the attack on Toronto (then called York) in the War of 1812, leaving to other men the task of exploring the ultimate reaches of the Mississippi.

In 1820 General Lewis Cass, governor of Michigan Territory, led an expedition in search of the river's source. His party, made up of a few engineers and a score of Indians, set out from Detroit in canoes; though the Great Lakes' pioneer steamboat, *Walk-in-the-Water*, was running to Mackinac, the Indians were afraid of the smoke-puffing craft and refused to board her. So the exploring party paddled the length of Lake Huron, portaged around the St. Mary's rapids and then paddled west along the wild shores of Lake Superior. They ascended the St. Louis River, past the site of the present city of Duluth, and made the Sandy River portage into the Mississippi. Thus they entered the river near the northernmost point reached by Pike's expedition fourteen years before. With their Indian guides and paddlers they penetrated the wandering river to a sky-blue lake rimmed in pine and cedar forest. The Indians called it "Ga-misquawakokag saigaiigun." Though he was generally fond of the native names, young Henry Schoolcraft, the mineralogist in Cass's party, quickly changed this designation to Cass Lake. General Cass learned from the Indians in the region that the Mississippi had its source in Elk Lake, a small body of water lying in the swamps and forests to the west. He took their word for it and headed his expedition home.

Even in those years, before steamboats carried travelers from Europe up the impressive valley, the Mississippi was known to Europeans as one of the great and legend-haunted rivers of the world. In Italy a one-time officer in the Italian Army, a gentleman and adventurer, had dreamed of discovering the true source of the Mississippi. Today the name of Giacomo Constantine Beltrami is written on the map of Minnesota, being given to a large county at the headwaters of the river.

When he reached America in 1823 Beltrami immediately traveled up the Mississippi to Fort Snelling, where he persuaded Major Stephen H. Long to let him accompany an expedition about to begin the survey of the Minnesota-Canada boundary. At the border he left the Long party and struck out with three Chippewa guides through the wilderness, traveling southeast toward the region in which he believed the Mississippi rose. When they were fired upon by a party of Sioux, his Indian companions deserted him and Beltrami was left alone somewhere on the Red Lake River. He toiled on to Red Lake, where he engaged a half-breed who helped him to discover a small heart-shaped lake in the middle of which the water boiled up mysteriously. This lake he named Lake Julia for a past romance (he said the lady was no longer living) and its water he conceived to filtrate through its banks both northward and southward. Thus in Lake Julia he believed that he had discovered the most southern source of the Red River of the North and the most northern source of the Mississippi. Later surveys proved that Lake Julia belongs entirely to the Red River basin.

Beltrami was satisfied, however, that he had realized his dream. When he wrote his account of it be grouped himself with Marco Polo, Columbus, the Cabots and other immortal discoverers. So he went triumphantly down the river and proceeded in New Orleans to publish *La decouverte des sources du Mississippi et de la rivière Sanglante; description du cours entier du Mississippi . . . ainsi que du cours entier de l'Ohio*. The book reveals an abundance of classical learning and a fondness for rhetorical grandeur. Beltrami had the excitement of a discoverer, if not his responsibility.

The true source of the river remained to be discovered, and the discovery fell to the lot of a man whose name adds dignity and color to the long story of men against the northern wilderness. Henry Rowe Schoolcraft was a scholar as well as an explorer, a man of deeply reflective mind and cultivated taste whose mission it was for twenty years to thread the forests and travel the wilderness rivers, seeking to bridge the gulf between the white man and the Indian. He began his career as an explorer in the mineral regions of Arkansas and Missouri, and though he was still in his early twenties his observations were so accurate and his report of the expedition so impressive that he was commissioned to join General Cass's party in its search for the Mississippi's source. Two years later, in 1822, Schoolcraft took up his quarters at Sault Ste. Marie as Indian agent on the northwest frontiers. He married a half-Indian wife, the granddaughter of a Chippewa chief, and with her help he devoted himself to an understanding of the Algonquin mind and its intricate, fear-haunted, sometimes beautiful mythology. His studies of the Indian language made a path for many ethnologists to follow and his *Algic Researches* opened the door of Indian folklore to the author of *Hiawatha*. With Schoolcraft's pages before him in his Cambridge study Henry Wadsworth Longfellow could see the gloom of Minnesota's forests and the gleam of the Big Sea Water and the lodges of the Chippewas huddled in the wilderness. But Schoolcraft's labors were not confined to ethnological research. He traveled to convocations of the tribes in the remote interior country and made Indian treaties that brought the United States vast and rich territory. He canoed down dark rivers and toiled over portage trails. Though he wrote poetry in his journals, he knew the north country like a voyageur.

In 1830 Schoolcraft was ordered to the Upper Mississippi to put an end (once more) to the hostilities between the Chippewas and the Sioux. He set out for the region that he had penetrated with Cass ten years earlier, but low water in the rivers made it impossible to enter the upper reaches of the Mississippi and he was forced to be content with holding Indian conferences on the St. Croix and Chippewa Rivers.

Again in 1832 the War Department ordered him to pursue that mission. To accomplish both a diplomatic and a geographical purpose he organized a party of thirty men and set out from the Soo to visit the Minnesota tribes and map the source of the Mississippi. In the company were Lieutenant James Allen and ten soldiers detailed for topographical survey, George Johnston, a Chippewa half-breed who was to serve as interpreter, the Reverend William T. Boutwell, a missionary to the northwestern Indians, and a slight youth, just twenty-three years old, named Douglass Houghton, who was attached to the party as surgeon and botanist.

Within a few years the name of Douglass Houghton was to loom large in the Northwest and it was to be remembered long after his death in the numbing waters of Lake Superior.

Now, in 1832, he was at the beginning of a brief and crowded career. The year before, he had come from the East to the busy frontier town of Detroit as a physician and a teacher of science. He looked even more boyish than his years, and his clients called him "Bub." Ten years later he was mayor of Detroit and had declined the presidency of the University of Michigan. In the years between 1837 and 1845 he made extensive surveys of the wild Upper Peninsula of Michigan. His strength was meager and his health was frail, but he explored every mile of the southern shore of Lake Superior and he mapped the mineral resources of a region that was to have an epic history. His reports drew men to that remote and rugged country. When he was drowned in an autumn storm off Keweenaw Peninsula, the Copper Country was already known in banking houses of New York and Boston and in financial circles across the Atlantic. On that bright June day in 1832 when he joined Schoolcraft's party at the foot of Lake Superior, his eyes were lighted with excitement. It was his first glimpse of the northern woods and waters.

Under fine June skies the party journeyed along the shore of Lake Superior. They paddled up the St. Louis River, following the route that Schoolcraft had taken with Cass twelve years earlier, and portaged into the Sandy River, entering the Mississippi on July 4th. They found a good flow of water in the river and passed without undue difficulty through Grand Rapids, Pokegama Falls, and the spacious Lake Winnibigoshish. At Cass Lake, Schoolcraft selected sixteen of his men, including Allen, Houghton, Boutwell, Johnston, three Indians, seven engineers and a cook, to go on to the source of the river, with a Chippewa named Ozawindeb, "Yellow Head," to serve as guide.

With five canoes this party pressed on. They found the river opening after thirty miles onto the blue expanse of Lake Bemidji, and there they turned southward, ascending an east fork of the Mississippi now known both as the Yellowhead and the Schoolcraft. After two days of toilsome progress the narrowing stream would no longer support their loaded craft. Heading southwest they made a long portage "of thirteen pauses," about six miles, and at its end Schoolcraft suddenly came upon a hill-girt, forest-fringed lake, blue as the summer sky. It was Itasca Lake, the true source of the Mississippi: it was the "Elk Lake" the Indians had described to General Cass and which the French from similar Indian accounts had named Lac la Biche, but whose location and contours had never been measured and which no white man, save perhaps a wandering fur trader, had ever seen. Where its two upper arms came together the lake enclosed a single island and there Schoolcraft camped on July 13, 1832. The lake Schoolcraft named Itasca, and Elk Lake became the name of the smaller one, a few miles south, which sends a tiny stream into it.

> Having gratified our curiosity in Itasca Lake [Schoolcraft wrote in his *Narrative* of the expedition], we prepared to leave the island, but did not feel inclined to quit the scene without leaving some memorial, however frail, of our visit. The men were directed to fell a few trees at the head of the island, thereby creating an area, for the purpose of erecting a flag staff. This was braced by forked stakes, and a small flag hoisted to its place. Taking specimens of the forest growth of the island of a size suitable for walking canes, and adding a few species to our collection of plants and conchology, we embarked on our descent. The flag which we had erected continued to be in sight for a time, and was finally shut out from our view by a curve of the lake.

Now Itasca Lake is the center of Itasca State Park, one of the most beautifully preserved areas of wilderness in all the North, and the name Itasca is more widely known than Schoolcraft could possibly have foreseen. But it is still the subject of controversy. Certain ethnologists have declared that Itasca is an Indian name, as indeed it sounds, and one of them, Mrs. Mary H. Eastman, published in 1853 a Chippewa legend of Itasca,

the sky-daughter of the tribal god Nanabozho, whose falling tears formed the rivulets which feed the lake. This story Mrs. Eastman said was told to her by School-craft himself, who got it from Yellow Head, his Chippewa guide. Schoolcraft's *Summary Narrative* of the expedition states that the Indian name for the lake was Omushkös, the Chippewa word for Elk.

After Schoolcraft's death, the Reverend William T. Boutwell supplied another explanation for the name. He said that one afternoon while making their slow canoe journey westward on Lake Superior, when the river's source was an anticipation in their minds, Schoolcraft had asked him for a classical word that would indicate the head or true source of a river. Boutwell offered *Verum Caput,* or the two Latin nouns *veritas* and *caput,* as his best suggestion. Schoolcraft busied himself with pencil and paper. A few minutes later he said, "I have got the thing," and showed Boutwell the word "Itasca" which he had coined by using syllables from the two Latin words.

Several other explanations have been offered from the Chippewa and Sioux languages, and the question remained unsettled when in 1932 was held the centennial celebration of Schoolcraft's discovery. Certain corroborations indicated that Schoolcraft might logically have coined a name from a combination of words: it was known that his name for Star Island, now a summer resort in Cass Lake, was Colcaspi, a conglomerate made from the names of the three explorers, Pike, Cass and Schoolcraft. It was also known that a few years after the Mississippi expedition he served on a commission that gave Indian names to Michigan's northern counties and that he was opposed to removing the native names from the American landscape. So the controversy over the name Itasca could continue. But a final confirmation of Boutwell's story has come with the discovery, by William J. Petersen of the State Historical Society of Iowa, of a letter written by Schoolcraft to the editor of a Galena newspaper shortly after the party had arrived at Fort Snelling on their return from the river's source. Wrote Schoolcraft: ". . . We made a portage of 6 miles, with our canoes, into La Biche or Itasca Lake (from a derivation of the expression *veritas caput*) which is the true source of this celebrated stream."

One other "explorer" should be mentioned, not because he added anything to men's knowledge of the river but because he, like many other Americans of each succeeding generation, felt the spell of the river and wanted to travel its entire course in his own craft. Captain Glazier, however, did not take his trip as a schoolboy on vacation, or as a newspaperman gathering material, or as a writer with a book in his head. He styled himself an "explorer"; he wanted his name to be coupled with the Mississippi. Since his historic voyage he has been laughed at, but he has been remembered.

Captain Willard Glazier, a veteran of the Civil War, turned to a career as professional adventurer, using his exploits as the subject of writings and lectures for American audiences in the seventies and eighties. He had already ridden across the continent on horseback, and had reaped what profit he could from that exploit, when he decided to "explore" the source of the Mississippi (he knew that Schoolcraft had not traveled the final five miles to Elk Lake, though the region had been thoroughly surveyed by Glazier's time) and to make the first *complete* journey down the river to its mouth.

Accordingly in the summer of 1881, with two companions and a pair of Indian paddlers, he began his undertaking at Leech Lake, striking west through the wooded country toward Lake Itasca. Though the mosquitoes were bad and after a couple of days the food was low in their haversacks, Glazier was filled with great expectations as he meditated upon the objective of his journey. "To stand at the SOURCE; to look upon the remotest rills and springs which contribute to the birth of the Great River of North America; to write *finis* in the volume opened by the renowned De Soto, more than three hundred years ago, and in which Marquette, La Salle, Hennepin, LaHontan, Carver, Pike, Beltrami, Schoolcraft and Nicollet have successively inscribed their names, were quite enough to revive the drooping spirits of the most depressed," he wrote in his subsequent volume *Down the Great River: embracing an account of the discovery of the True Source of the Mississippi, together with views, descriptive and pictorial, of the cities, towns, villages and villages and scenery on the banks of the river, as seen during a canoe voyage of over three thousand miles from its head waters to the Gulf of Mexico.* A good book deserves a good title, and Captain Glazier did not slight his.

He named his canoe the *Discovery.* In that craft he paddled through water grass and rushes into an oval of pure and tranquil water about a mile and a half in length. This lake Glazier recognized as the true source of the Mississippi and it moved him greatly. Later, in

his book, and without using quotation marks, he transferred the account of Schoolcraft's first glimpse of Lake
Itasca to his first view of Elk Lake, which he named
Lake Glazier. At the time, he made a speech to his companions and, though he had said that the party was
hungry and out of ammunition, he reported that they
fired volleys of commemoration. His book pictures him
standing cross-armed in a birch canoe while gazing on
the scene of his discovery.

Then he set out on his voyage. "Now for the Gulf
of Mexico!" he exclaimed, and they were on their way.
But the path of the explorer must not be too smooth.
Captain Glazier named his first camp, on the shores of
Lake Glazier, "Camp Discovery." However the excitement of making history was tempered by the "gnawings
of hunger," despite the fact that they were in midsummer with two Indian guides in the midst of one of the
richest fishing grounds in all the North. To make his
plight more serious the captain refused the Indians' sug-
gestions of portaging to save time and distance, because
he was determined to paddle his canoe the *entire* course
of the Mississippi. Camp Discovery was followed by
"Camp Otter," where the hungry party feasted on a
roast otter which the captain shot from his canoe, a feat
for which the two Indian guides "unanimously" voted
him "a great hunter." But Camp Otter was followed
by "Camp Hunger," and that by "Camp Starvation."
This extreme point in the fortunes of the Glazier expedition was reached in the woods twenty miles above
Lake Bemidji on July 25th; that evening the captain
had to be helped out of his canoe, being too weak to
walk without assistance. But the next stop became

"Camp Relief," by virtue of their meeting an Indian family in a canoe who sold the explorers dried fish and maple sugar.

At Lake Winnibigoshish the Indian guides left the party. Standing on the shore Captain Glazier "addressed" them, recounting the leading incidents of the journey, describing the discovery they had made and the privations they had been called upon to endure. He thanked them for their part in the success of the undertaking and presented them with his photograph. With a final handshake he parted from his Indian colleagues.

At Brainard, then the first town of consequence on the river, Captain Glazier gave the first lecture on his trip. This activity became a feature of his progress down the river. He sent an advance agent ahead of him to announce the imminent arrival of the explorer and to arrange lecture engagements. His lecture, "Pioneers of the Mississippi," recounted the efforts of a long list of explorers and narrated his own experience in finding the river's ultimate source. Frequently his advance agent had a delegation assembled at the river landing to cheer when Glazier appeared around the bend. At the most hospitable towns whistles shrilled, bands played, people lined the shore, and representatives of the local press came out to meet him in skiffs and rowboats.

So Captain Willard Glazier passed triumphantly down the Mississippi, as have done many others, and after a journey of 117 days, on the afternoon of November 15, 1881, the prow of his canoe met the salt waves of the Gulf.

PART TWO

The Expanding Nation

CHAPTER 5

A Fort in the Wilderness

THERE are places on the Upper Mississippi where the past has remained though the present eddies around it like currents of water. Remember the crumbling old town of Prairie du Chien above the Wisconsin River's mouth, or the grave of Julien Dubuque on the quiet hilltop above the spacious valley. Or picture the ivy-mantled tower of Fort Snelling among the elm trees that were planted long ago, the parapet rising like a castle on an Old World river and looking across the roofs and towers of St. Paul.

Crowning the most picturesque and commanding site on the whole length of the river, Fort Snelling stands on the precipitous and narrowing bluff above the meeting of the Minnesota and the Mississippi. From the first, when it was only a wild headland in the wilderness, traders recognized its dominance and explorers foresaw the strategic function it would one day have in controlling the trade and communication of the north country. So young Lieutenant Pike had shrewdly acquired title to it in 1805, years before the government had any thought of planting a garrison in so remote a place.

It was still remote in 1819 when Lieutenant Colonel Henry Leavenworth was dispatched up the Mississippi to establish a military post at the mouth of the St.

Peter's (formerly the St. Pierre, now the Minnesota) River. Only after Leavenworth was on his way was it remembered that the Indians had never been paid the full price agreed upon in their treaty with Pike; there was a matter of two thousand dollars in trade goods still undelivered. So Major Thomas Forsyth, the Indian agent down the river at Rock Island, ascended the Mississippi with Leavenworth's troops carrying trade goods to be distributed among the tribes. He divided his wares among six chiefs, including Wabasha, Red Wing, Little Crow, and Shakopee, to be distributed among their people. As a bonus, or to make the government's amends for the long delay in payment, he gave each of the bands a small stock of whisky. Thus they received indulgently his announcement that the Great Father was about to erect a fort at the mouth of the St. Peter's. He explained that this would be a benefit to the tribes, as it would provide them with a blacksmith shop and a trading center. However, he added, as a precautionary word, that by a single blow on his whistle the Great Father could summon to the projected fort as many soldiers as he pleased.

When Colonel Leavenworth arrived the forests rang with sounds never before heard in that north country. Axes thudded at the base of hardwood trees, the leafy crowns crashed down and the rough timbers were hewn while oak and maple chips snowed on the ground. Pine logs, floated down from the Rum River, were sawed by hand into building lumber. Then there was a clatter of hammers through the summer weeks while the first rough buildings rose on that bold point of land.

When the barracks had been erected Colonel Leavenworth was relieved by Colonel Josiah Snelling, a

veteran of the War of 1812, who retained command for seven years. He was a brusque, convivial man, improvident, generous, a lover of good horses and good whisky. He set up a sawmill beside the Falls of St. Anthony and proceeded with the enlargement of the barracks and fortifications. When General Scott inspected the post in 1824 he was so impressed by the commandant's efficiency that he recommended the change of its name from Fort St. Anthony to Fort Snelling.

The fort in the wilderness had a twofold purpose, to protect the fur trade and to control the Indians. Soon after his arrival Colonel Snelling had evidence of the need for such an outpost. One autumn day in 1823 his soldiers brought in to the fort a six-year-old child, John Tully, whom they had secured from a band of Sioux. The child had been carried away by the Indians after they had murdered his father, his mother, and his infant brother. John himself had been scalped; he carried a fresh pink scar on the crown of his tow-colored head. Colonel Snelling adopted the orphaned boy and he lived in the fort until his death, from an infection, four years later.

Colonel Snelling had a gentleman's tastes. In his diary, references to lumber wagons, log chains, and harness are mixed with such items as coral earrings, French china, and silver spoons. Though the post was hundreds of miles from civilization, the wives of the officers made it a place of social life and ceremony, alongside the traffic of red men stalking in their blankets to barter furs at the sutler's store and men in blue drilling on the parade grounds. There were winter nights when the rough board tables of the mess hall groaned under huge pots of pork and beans, whole roast hams and beef tongues, mounds of doughnuts and steaming kettles of coffee, rows of cakes and pies. After the quadrilles and the Virginia reels the men tramped back to their barracks. In the moonlight the bugler stood rigid as a flagstaff and between the snowy hills, over the icebound rivers, the notes rang cold and clear.

In the 1820's there was a flood of commerce on the Lower Mississippi, steamers, barges, flatboats, and keelboats endlessly passing between the mouth of the Ohio and the proud city of New Orleans. But above the Ohio the Mississippi valley was a wilderness and the vacant river dreamed on between its shores as it had done for ages. Cairo was a place of two buildings, a log cabin and a warehouse for the keelboatmen's stores. St. Louis was a town of two thousand with an occasional steamer smoking at its primitive levee. The site of Quincy showed one rude cabin where John Woods, later governor of Illinois, was clearing bottom land. At Hannibal the only settler was John S. Miller, a blacksmith who shortly moved to Galena at the news of the lead smelting. Fort Madison was a ghost barracks above the river, having been erected in 1808 and abandoned five years later. The trading post of Julien Dubuque had grown up with prairie grass after his death in 1810. There was no sign on the cloud-shadowed riverbanks of the modern cities of Moline, Burlington, Davenport, La Crosse.

But civilization was destined to come up the river, in the form of a puffing steamboat. Under the bright skies of May, 1823, the stern-wheeler *Virginia*, with Captain John Crawford in command, took her way up the uncharted channel, between the bluffs and the wooded shores, past the many islands and the mouths of northern rivers. She was the first steam vessel to stain the skies over Lake Pepin and to tremble in the current below St. Anthony's Falls.

Among the passengers on the *Virginia* was the explorer Beltrami, who displayed his classical learning in his description of the Indians' fright as the little steamboat passed under Fort Snelling. "I know not what impression the first sight of the Phoenician vessels might make on the inhabitants of the coast of Greece; or the Triremi of the Romans on the wild natives of Iberia, Gaul or Britain; but I am sure it could not be stronger than that which I saw on the countenance of the savages at the arrival of our steamboat."

Another passenger was Major Lawrence Taliaferro, the Indian agent at Fort Snelling, who was returning from a business trip to St. Louis. An able and magnetic man, he understood the Indians' love of ceremony, oratory, and gaudy apparel, and by employing this knowledge he impressed the savages with his own importance. Many American officials envied and hated him, as much for his success in a difficult office as for his vanity and egotism. But the Indians, with all their tribal feuds and jealousies, called him "Four Hearts" in tribute to the impartiality with which he conducted his affairs. For a generation he exercised great influence with the tribes on the Upper Mississippi.

With the arrival of the *Virginia* at Fort Snelling, Major Taliaferro (pronounced to rhyme with "Gulliver") must have realized that new problems were at hand. Goods for the fur trade came up the river from St. Louis every season and were stored in the roomy warehouse of the American Fur Company at Mendota, until the Indians and traders arrived with their winter's catch of peltry. Now that a steamer had found the way to that remote place, the Upper Mississippi tribes would be much closer to the civilization of the white man. Such harmless articles as pans and kettles, mirrors and tobacco would lose their power over the savages. Guns and powder would replace their primitive implements of hunting and of war. And whisky would arrive with the smoke of every steamboat.

At the northern posts traders found it necessary, though they knew it was unwise, to furnish whisky to the Indians; if they refused, whole tribes would carry their furs to the border where Canadian traders were waiting with an ample stock. There was no way for Colonel Snelling or Major Taliaferro to control the dispensing of spirits outside the military reservation. So the Indians flocked to rude taverns on the east bank of the river, and the soldiers from the fort provided further custom. A familiar punishment for such offenders from the barracks was to march the man under guard up and down the reservation grounds with his head and arms thrust through a barrel labeled "I Was Drunk Last Night." But the fear of disgrace was no deterrent when a man craved the good quick fire of whisky and often there were not enough barrels to go around. On one night forty-seven of the garrison were in the guardhouse for that offense.

After 1832 steamboats arrived at Fort Snelling with regularity, bringing tourists as well as merchants, army officers and pioneer settlers. One of the early western travelers, who left a rich record of his visits, was the artist George Catlin. He spent several seasons on the Upper Mississippi and painted more than six hundred scenes of Indian life, including portraits, games, villages, tribal dances, and religious ceremonies. The wilderness fascinated Catlin as much as its aborigines. In the summer of 1835 he floated down the river in a canoe, painting many striking landscapes of the Upper Mississippi. He became the most effective advertiser of the early steamboat routes and the thrills which they offered to travelers from the East. In fact, Catlin outlined a Fashionable Tour which involved a trip by the Ohio River to St. Louis, thence up the Mississippi to the Falls of St. Anthony, returning to Prairie du Chien and crossing the state of Wisconsin to Green Bay and then back to the East on a Great Lakes steamer by way of Mackinac, Detroit, and Niagara. In the middle years of the century thousands of Americans took this "fashionable tour," and among them were many travelers from England and the Continent.

Fort Snelling was the ultimate point of the tour and to many travelers it was the climax as well. Carriages clattered over the roads taking tourists to see the Falls of St. Anthony, which steamers could not approach except in seasons of extreme low water. Trails led through the woods to Minnehaha Falls pouring over a ledge in a forest glen a short distance from the Mississippi. On the grassy plain above the river gorge travelers could visit the picturesque camp of the Red River half-breeds, with their oxen and tame buffalo grazing beside their famous two-wheeled carts. Down on the riverbank Pierre Battineau, a reckless half-breed trader, was always ready to amuse people by skipping silver dollars across the Mississippi. The trading compound of the Fur Company and the camps of the Indians quickened the eye of tourists, and carriages waited to take them up the steep road to the fort where men in blue marched with their sabers glinting in the sun.

Even then, with its castellated tower crowning the precipitous height above the rivers, Fort Snelling had the air of a storied place. As time went on, its traditions grew. High army officers reviewed the troops on the drill ground and the cannon salute boomed for visiting dignitaries.

An unexpected person in that northern outpost was the most famous Negro slave in the history of America. Dred Scott, a slave owned by Joseph Emerson, assistant surgeon of the United States Army, had accompanied his master from Missouri to Fort Snelling when Dr. Emerson was named medical officer of the post. Though a freed man, as slavery had been prohibited in that region, the Negro was still attached to Dr. Emerson as a servant. In 1837 in the Round Tower of the fort Dred Scott was married to a Negro girl, who also had been a slave in the service of Dr. Emerson. Two years later Dr. Emerson returned to Missouri, taking the two ex-slaves with him. In 1848 Dred Scott sued for his freedom, on the ground that having once been freed he had acquired a permanent status of a free man. Thus began one of the most famous cases in the judicial history of the United States.

Another unexpected resident at Fort Snelling was Count Zeppelin, who served in his youth as a military attaché to the United States and fought for a time with the Union Army in the Civil War. In 1862 he was sent to the northwestern frontier and was given quarters in the Round Tower of Fort Snelling. There, in his middle twenties, he carried on experiments with captive balloons, and on a calm spring evening in 1864 he made his first flight. His balloon, constructed of canvas and filled with illuminating gas, rose three hundred feet above the military grounds and drifted for thirty minutes over the Mississippi. Unfortunately no one reported the Indians' reaction to that spectacle.

The campaigns of the Civil War were fought far from Minnesota, but in 1862 the Sioux, shrewdly timing their move when thousands of soldiers had gone to the white man's war, staged their great uprising. Sweeping across the upper Minnesota River, they slaughtered four hundred persons and ambushed a company of soldiers before an army of volunteer defenders met and withstood them at New Ulm. At a subsequent military trial, three hundred of the Sioux were condemned to death. President Lincoln commuted the sentence of all but thirty-nine, however, taking the stand that those who had merely fought in open battle should be treated as prisoners of war. As a result of the uprising all Sioux annuities were canceled and title to their reservation lands was annulled.

In the autumn of 1862 two of the Sioux leaders in the bloody revolt were brought to Fort Snelling for execution. There under guard they walked the compound, each dragging a cannon ball chained to his foot. Medicine Bottle was a coarse, ugly fellow who defiantly showed to visitors his arm tattooed with symbols indicating the men, women and children he had scalped— fully fifty in all. Shakopee, or Little Six, was a Sioux of different temper. He had been a shrewd, bold chief; he was dignified as he faced his death. The scaffold had been built on a knoll commanding the hills across the Minnesota River and Pilot Knob, now the Acacia Cemetery. When Shakopee stood there in the autumn sunlight with the black cape about to go over his head, a locomotive whistle shrilled under the bluff. It was the first steam train pulling into Mendota.

With a dramatic hand Shakopee pointed across the river. His voice filled the execution ground: "As the white man comes in the Indian goes out." Then the trap door fell and Shakopee swung gently in the wind.

With the coming of the railroad the fort's great days were over. For more than thirty years it had been the farthest army post on the northwestern frontier. But in 1858 Minnesota became a sovereign state and the territorial period was ended. Four years later the railroad linked it to the expanding life of the nation. Fort Snelling was to linger on, more significant in its past than its present, to grow old, its elm trees arching and its tower softened with ivy. Now the color guard wears copies of the regiment's first uniforms and the storied Round Tower has been converted into a museum of Minnesota history.

CHAPTER 6

Black Hawk's Last Stand

O N A rich tableland three miles south of Rock Island lay the chief village of the Sac Indians. Here, in a picturesque setting between the Rock River and the Mississippi, was the center of their tribal life, their national cemetery, and the 3,000-acre field of corn and pumpkins which yielded their principal food supply. From the village, eastward, ran the great Sac Trail, the most important aboriginal highway in Illinois, striking straight across the prairie to the southern tip of Lake Michigan and continuing through Michigan Territory to Detroit. Westward, across the Mississippi, were the prairie groves of Iowa which made up the traditional hunting grounds of the Sac tribesmen. Though the village numbered no more than five hundred families, it was one of the strongest and largest Indian towns in North America.

In the dark summer of 1832 this small plot of ground above the Mississippi, a few square miles of domesticated earth amid a great sweep of empty country, became the cause of a foolish and tragic war. At the outset the controversy could have been settled for the price of six thousand dollars; Black Hawk would have withdrawn his people across the river for that paltry payment. Later the bloodshed could have been averted by accepting the Indians' surrender; three times the Sac chief sent his men out of the woods under a white flag of truce. But a fever had possessed the entire Middle Border. Tales of Indian savagery went like a wind across the country until troops were summoned and expeditions mounted to hunt the tribesmen down and drive them forever beyond the Mississippi. Far away from the Sac village, in the port of Buffalo, four ships were loaded with troops and supplies for the Black Hawk campaign. In Illinois, Governor Reynolds issued three fiery proclamations calling for a powerful force of volunteers to aid the regulars from the frontier garrisons. In the end, when the Sac village lay in ruin and the Sac women huddled in hunger around their dead on the river shore, the campaign had cost two million dollars and four hundred needless lives.

The story of Black Hawk's War is the darkest chapter of American enterprise on the Upper Mississippi. It begins darkly, with an ambiguous and grasping Indian treaty; it developed with cruelty and with pointless fear and hatred; it ends with the massacre of people who only sought to till their own ancestral fields and preserve their traditional burying ground.

The Indians were shortsighed, as befits a people who depend each season on the fortunes of their hunt and the harvest of their crudely cultivated fields. So in 1804, when there were no white settlers anywhere in the wild domain of the Sac and Fox tribes, a loosely confederated people, the tribesmen saw no reason to refuse an annuity of three thousand dollars in return for the cession of some fifty million acres of land, including the territory north of the Illinois River, south of the Wisconsin, and east of the Mississippi. There was a further induce-

ment in the terms: the United States government stipu-
lated that as long as the lands remained public domain
the Indians should enjoy the privilege of living and
hunting upon them. No Sac Indian knew land as any
other kind of property than public domain; it looked
like an annuity for nothing and of course they signed
the treaty. Within the ceded area was the Sac village on
the V of land between the Rock River and the Mississippi.

For twenty years the Sac treaty was merely one
more document filed away in the government offices at
Washington. But in the summer of 1823 restless bands
of squatters pushing ahead of the homestead areas in
Illinois found the fertile fields of the Sac village ready
to be planted to a white man's crop. At that time the
extreme line of settlement open to sale and occupation
lay some sixty miles to the east, the country between
that frontier and the Mississippi not having been surveyed. Consequently, squatters had no rights in the territory. Even then, the Indians would have been tractable
had the squatters taken a fancy to any other region than
the land about the Sac village. In his famous autobiography, dictated to an interpreter while he was a prisoner
of war, Black Hawk asserted that his people proposed
to give up any other land, even their lead mines, "to be
peaceably permitted to keep the small point of land on
which our village was situated."

But in all that empty country it was the rich
alluvial plain between the two rivers that the squatters
wanted. They proceeded to fence in small areas of the
Indian fields, to whip squaws and children who ventured
beyond those bounds, even to burn outlying lodges of

the Sac town. Each winter the Indians left their village to go on their annual hunt. When they returned in the spring they found their village plundered and their cemetery under the plow of the squatters.

Black Hawk appealed to the Indian agent at Fort Armstrong, located on Rock Island in the Mississippi, and was advised to move his people permanently across the river. At this point the chief affirmed, in contradiction to the terms of subsequent agreements he had signed, that in the treaty of 1804 the tribes had never ceded the land on which the Sac village stood. In this claim he was supported by his Indian advisers and by the British authorities at Fort Malden, across the Detroit River, who were anxious to foment Indian trouble on the frontier of the United States. Later Black Hawk explained in his autobiography:

> I heard that there was a great chief on the Wabash, and sent a party to get his advice. They informed him that we had not sold our village. He assured them, then, that if we had not sold the land on which our village stood, our Great Father would not take it from us. I started early to Malden to see the chief of my British Father and told him my story. He gave me the same reply that the chief on the Wabash had given me. . . . I next called on the great chief at Detroit, and made the same statement to him that I had to the chief of our British Father. He gave me the same reply. . . . This assured me that I was right, and determined me to hold out, as I had promised our people.

Thus Black Hawk took the stand that was to give his name a place, though a tragic one, in history. He was at this time a man past sixty years of age, a short, lean man, quiet in his bearing, with fine strong eyes, and a long tufted scalp lock flaunting an eagle feather. His full name was Makataimeshekiakiak, or Black Sparrow Hawk, and though not a hereditary chief he was by common consent the leader of his people. He was restless, ambitious, easily influenced, though he appears to have been honest in his love of the Sac traditional "home" and his concern over the perpetuation of their burying ground. After the struggle was over he put his motives into dignified and unimpeachable words: "Rock River was a beautiful country. I liked my town, my cornfields, and the home of my people. I fought for them."

When, after a meager winter's hunt, the Sacs returned to the village in the spring in 1831, they found the squatters in entire possession of their town. The Indian lodges were pillaged and their graveyard was furrowed with fresh plowing. On being warned to keep his people away, Black Hawk responded that it was the newcomers who must vacate that site. This announcement, exaggerated as it traveled, reached the ears of Governor Reynolds, who promptly called up sixteen hundred volunteers to march to the scene with ten companies of regulars under General Edmund P. Gaines, commander of the Western Army. Confronted by such a force, the Indians withdrew to the west bank of the Mississippi, where they agreed never to return to the Illinois side of the river.

But the Sac spirits were smoldering. They passed a wretched, hungry summer, without a crop to harvest, staring bitterly across to the fertile fields and desecrated graveyards of their home. That winter they plotted with the tribesmen of the Winnebagos, Ottawas, Chippewas and Potawatomis for a general Indian uprising. In April, 1832, the Sacs crossed the Mississippi and journeyed up the Rock River to the chief town of the Winnebagos, where they planned to raise a crop of corn and prepare for a campaign in the fall.

When news of the Sac invasion of Illinois reached Governor Reynolds, he called for another levy of volunteers. General Henry Atkinson sent messengers to Black Hawk, ordering him to withdraw immediately to the west bank of the Mississippi. Black Hawk answered with defiance. A force of sixteen hundred men then set out to overwhelm the Sacs. A restless and reckless battalion under Major Isaiah Stillman pushed ahead, fresh on the trail of the retreating Indians. At word of their approach Black Hawk, who had discovered that the Winnebagos and Potawatomis would not join his war after all, sent three men under a flag of truce to convey his offer to meet General Atkinson in council. But Stillman's troopers were hungry for action. They rushed out and captured the envoys, carrying them back to camp as prisoners of war. Black Hawk had sent five more Sacs to watch the reception of the truce-bearers. When these braves were discovered, Stillman's men gave chase. Three of the Sacs reached Black Hawk's camp and reported the death of two of their number and of the three original envoys. The chief himself had been preparing a flag of truce under which he planned to approach the white forces. Now he tore the flag to pieces and called upon the forty men in his party to avenge their brothers' blood.

There were three hundred men in Stillman's company, but when the handful of Sacs darted from behind a screen of brush they thought themselves attacked by a superior number. So the first grotesque encounter ended with three hundred men in desperate flight. They left everything behind them, plunging their horses through swamps and creeks, some of them not stopping till they reached their own homes many miles away. On their abandoned campsite the Indians were busy gathering up stores of food and ammuntion. Fifty miles away the frightened, undisciplined troopers, still looking over their shoulders, told a breathless tale of two thousand savages sweeping furiously across all of northern Illinois.

The story of Stillman's defeat ran like a wind through the West. Suddenly Black Hawk became a name for cruelty and terror. Men ran panic-stricken from their fields at the innocent sound of cattle trampling the brush or of a wild turkey gobbling in the forest. Hundreds of families fled from their homes and all along the frontier tales of the Indians' ferocity grew. It was the worst case of jitters in all the history of the Middle Border. To make the story even more disgraceful, the volunteer militia refused to follow Black Hawk's trail north of the Illinois boundary, claiming that they had enlisted for but one month and that they were subject to service only within the state. They were disbanded, and Black Hawk had time to gather his forces for a stand in southern Wisconsin.

With this initial and stinging defeat of the white man's authority, General Winfield Scott ordered a thousand regulars to be transported from the East by way of the Great Lakes, and Governor Reynolds called for a new levy of two thousand men to serve for the dura-

tion of the war. Meanwhile spasmodic warfare spread
over northern Illinois, where small parties of Indians carried on scalping raids. In one such episode a party led by
Mike Girty, a renegade in the pay of the British, slaughtered fifteen men, women, and children who had gathered at the Davis farm on Indian Creek, north of the
town of Ottawa. Two daughters of William Hall, nine-
teen-year-old Sylvia and seventeen-tear-old Rachel,
were carried away alive. For eleven days the sisters remained captive, being taken north to Lake Koshkonong
where Black Hawk had dug in. There through the in-
tercession of Henry Gratiot, an Indian agent, and a neu-
tral Winnebago chief named White Crow, they were
ransomed for two thousand dollars in goods and horses.

By the middle of June, three weeks after Stillman's
rout, a force of more than four thousand men, militia
companies, territorial rangers, and regular infantry, was
in the field. Under General Atkinson a main army ad-
vanced toward Black Hawk's position at Lake Koshkonong while smaller forces pushed up the Mississippi to
cut off any Indian attempt to cross the river. When
General Atkinson reached Koshkonong he found the
Sacs gone. For days his troops floundered through the
swamps and forests of that region, exhausting themselves and their supplies without coming to grips with
the furtive enemy. At last they struck his trail, marked
by a litter of Indian mats, kettles and implements which
the Sacs had discarded in their haste. With fresh purpose
the troopers hurried on. Soon they were overtaking
stragglers, weak with hunger, from the Sac caravan.
They overtook the main body just short of the Wisconsin River. While a small Sac guard fought a delaying

action on the "Wisconsin Heights," the rest of the Indians succeeded in crossing the river.

Black Hawk was encumbered with the entire Sac populace, and at this juncture he sent a large party of old men, women, and children down the river on rafts and canoes begged from the Winnebagos. He hoped that these noncombatants would be allowed to descend the Wisconsin and cross the Mississippi in peace. But word was sent to the garrison at Fort Crawford, at the Wisconsin River's mouth. These brave soldiers fired on the fugitives in midstream, killing fifteen and capturing some forty of them. Many were drowned in the turmoil and those who escaped to the woods died of hunger or were massacred by a band of Menominee mercenaries under white leadership.

From Wisconsin Heights, Black Hawk's trail led north and west, through a rugged and difficult country, toward the Mississippi. General Atkinson's men pushed on over this hard terrain. On the way they found dead Sacs, who had succumbed to wounds or starvation, and they saw the fleeing savages were reduced to eating the flesh of their exhausted ponies and the bark of trees. So the troops toiled up the hillsides and floundered through the swamps, until from a last broken height they looked down upon the Bad Axe River flowing into the wide-curving Mississippi.

On the first day of August, Black Hawk had reached the Mississippi. Here with a few canoes and one large raft he attempted to get his wretched band across the river. In the midst of that frantic effort the army transport *Warrior*, under Captain John Throckmorten, steamed around the bend. The *Warrior* carried a com-

pany of United States regulars, and Black Hawk knew
quickly that his situation was hopeless. Accordingly, he
raised a white flag and told his men to lay down their
arms for a peaceable surrender. The response from the
Warrior was three rounds of canister shot, fired at close
range, which left a group of Indians writhing on the
shore. After a fusillade of musket fire the *Warrior* withdrew, proceeding down the river to Prairie du Chien.

That night a few Indians made their way across the
river, but Black Hawk with a small party fled east to a
hideout in the rocky dells of the Wisconsin. He was an
old man, knowing the bitterness of defeat and the end of
the free life of his people. Torn between the fear of a fu-
gitive and the responsibility of a leader, he returned the
next day and from a place of concealment on a Mississippi bluff he saw General Atkinson's men surrounding
his people in their final battle. It was a fight in the
ravines and bottom lands, a weird and hopeless struggle
among logs, trees, and underbrush. The Indians, weak
from hunger, fought desperately and died within a clos-
ing circle of gunfire. Some of them waded through the
shallows to Battle Island, but the *Warrior*, returning to
the scene, slaughtered them with broadsides from its
canister. Some swam desperately toward the west bank
of the Mississippi, but only a few survived the river currents and the deadly aim of Atkinson's sharpshooters to
crawl exhausted on the Iowa shore. There they joined
the miserable band who had made the crossing during
the night.

The Battle of Bad Axe lasted three hours. When it
was over, Black Hawk still stood on his bluff above the
Mississippi thinking the hard thoughts of disaster. In

the bright month of April he had led a thousand followers across the river to assert their right to the land
they had cultivated with their crude hoes and harrows
and consecrated with their dead. Now, four months
later, barely a hundred wretched fugitives had returned
to sanctuary across the Mississippi. With a sinking heart
the old chief turned back into the forest.

A few days later, after the war was ended, General Winfield Scott arrived at Prairie du Chien. His face
was lined and his eyes were troubled, as though still in
the toils of a bitter campaign. None of his thousand
regulars from the East had smelled the smoke of battle,
but one out of every four of them was dead. Cholera
had broken out on his troopship, striking swiftly after
they had embarked from Buffalo. One vessel, steaming
through the Detroit River with her death list growing,
put ashore at Fort Gratiot, just above Port Huron, to
evacuate the stricken. There the sick were carried ashore
and the rest of the terrified men fled through the fields
and woods of Michigan as though they could outdistance
that invisible enemy. Another transport arrived outside
the Chicago River with doom spreading through her
cabins. Sixteen of her troops were already dead and
buried in Lake Michigan. During the next five days
eighty-five more bodies slid into the water. Within a
few weeks cholera was raging all the way down the
Mississippi, traveling the great waterway, and people
died in St. Louis and New Orleans of a plague brought
to the western country by Black Hawk's tragic war.

For three weeks the desolate old chief hid in the
rocky fastness of the Wisconsin Dells. Then two Winnebagos led a party of American soldiers to the place and

Black Hawk was a prisoner of war. At Fort Crawford he was delivered to Colonel Zachary Taylor, later president of the United States, and shortly afterward in the custody of a young southern officer, Lieutenant Jefferson Davis, who was also to become a president, he was taken down the Mississippi to Jefferson Barracks. The following spring he was taken to Washington—and that proved a strangely triumphant journey for the beaten old chief, who found throngs of cheering people waiting for him in every city on the route. The white men were quick to forget their lurid tales of the fierce Hawk, now that his wings were clipped and his talons broken. They received him like a hero. Black Hawk could not grasp the doctrine of Manifest Destiny, and certainly he could not understand the irony of American folklore that cherishes the resisting chief ahead of the generals who were sent against him.

Back to a reservation on the Des Moines River went the old chief. There in 1838, seventy-one years of age, he died. But his name remained a legend in the Mississippi country. Within a year his body was stolen from its grave and put on exhibition in the towns of Illinois. On demand of the territorial governor of Iowa the skeleton was recovered and deposited in a law office in Iowa City, the new capital. On a cold winter night in 1853 the building burned to the ground. Then there was nothing left but the memory of a stubborn leader who took his people down a hopeless path of war.

Now on a bluff above the Rock River, overlooking the historic valley of the Sacs, stands the great stone statue of the defeated chief. It rises fifty feet above its massive pedestal, a majestic figure in an attitude of dignity and reflection, gazing over the land of his fathers. It is frankly idealized; that was the sculptor's conception. When the statue was completed, Lorado Taft wrote:

This is the way it happened. Every evening as the shadows turned blue we walked over this bluff. We always stopped at this point to rest. . . . As we stood here we involuntarily folded our arms and it came to me that generations before had done so. And so the figure grew out of the attitude, as we stood and looked on this beautiful scene. . . . I did not study any one race or type of Indians. It is a composite of the Foxes and the Sacs, the Sioux and the Mohawks, and, in short, it represents the Indian personality. I have left off the usual Indian trappings—the feather and buckskins and other conventional signs. There is even a hint of the old Roman in the face, which was necessary to make it suggest a spirit unconquered while still the conquered race.

It is an impressive statue, and it would puzzle the desolate old chief to see his memorial now standing heroically above the valley where the white men would not let his people tend their little strip of ground and honor the graves of their dead.

CHAPTER 7

The Creaking of Red River Carts

Two streams of commerce met on the river landings below St. Anthony's Falls. One came by water to the head of navigation and the other came by land from a wide, wild country hundreds of miles beyond the farthest reaches of the Mississippi.

On a fine summer Sunday in the pioneer church at St. Anthony, the minister had just intoned his text when a shrill, discordant noise broke in. The sound grew, filling the bare wooden room and drawing every pair of eyes in the congregation to the open windows. "This text will be discussed next Sunday," the preacher shouted while his voice could still be heard. Then he came down from his pulpit. The congregation streamed out after him to watch the passing of the Red River caravan.

The sound of the Red River carts announced their coming farther away than you could hear a steamboat's whistle, and that screeching racket helped to make them famous. The high-slung carts, each with a deep, slant-walled bed mounted on two solid disk wheels sawed from the round of a tree, were a wonder of axmanship. They were made entirely of wood, usually oak; the joints were secured by wooden pins and the wooden hubs complained on dry wooden axles. The wheels had rims three inches wide to carry the carts across marshes and rivers without miring. Occasionally rawhide was wrapped round the rims for tires, and the ox or tame buffalo was hitched to the cart with rawhide thongs. Into the deep bed the Red River men piled the furs from the Canadian country above Pembina and Fort Garry, a colorful variety of pelts ranging all the way from buffalo to beaver. In addition to their assorted peltry the caravans were laden with pemmican, moccasins, and dried buffalo tongues. A load was not complete until the wheels shrieked at every round.

The half-breed drivers were as picturesque a lot of men as the American frontier ever produced. Blond and swarthy faces, sky-blue eyes and eyes as black as night, red and sandy and raven hair, they showed all the variations which could be produced by a mingling of Indian and Caucasian blood. They wore coats of coarse blue cloth fastened with bone buttons, scarlet sashes, jaunty beaded caps, fringed leggings of deerskin, and beaded moccasins. They strode lightly on the balls of their feet, covering vast tracts of country with a tireless, fluid stride. Amid the ear-splitting chorus of their ungreased axles they sang songs from a Norman country they had never seen, of Isabeau taking a walk by the stream, of gay roses in May, of rolling a ball and plucking a lark, of Malbrouck gone to war, and a sweetheart's Sunday ribbons and other innocent and carefree themes. When an ox lunged out of the trail or a heavy wheel sank through the fresh spring sod they broke off singing for sudden torrents of profanity. They were tough, hard-bitten, reckless, lyrical men.

They had come a long way. Between the Mississippi and the Red River of the North ran the Red River Trail, used for thirty years by the Pembina caravans. The fur traders of the Lake Winnipeg country brought their peltry to St. Paul when that settlement was called Pig's Eye in honor of the one-eyed half-breed, Pierre Parrant, who kept a shanty saloon on the riverbank. Their first trips were made in dog sleds before the winter snow was gone, but when the volume of furs increased they built the Red River carts and sent them in mile-long caravans over the northern prairie. They had no road to follow but guided their 400-mile journey by a few landmarks— Traverse des Sioux, the south rim of Swan Lake, the mouth of the Cottonwood River, and Lac qui Parle. After a few seasons they found other routes and each year the drivers made their choice of the Woods Trail through the Crow Wing and Leaf River valleys and around the northeast shore of Otter Tail Lake and so to Pembina, or the Plains Trail which left the Mississippi at St. Cloud and struck across the prairie until it found the Red River at Breckenridge. Usually the larger caravans, comprising as many as two hundred carts, followed the longer Plains Trail which offered easier travel and abundant forage for their animals.

It was five weeks on the road for them and two weeks of noisy barter at their St. Paul camp on Larpenteur's Lake. They left Pembina in early summer, when golden clouds of coreopsis fringed the lagoons and the buffalo grass was high enough for good grazing. In August when the prairie nights were growing sharp and the smoke of their campfires was spicy in the evening air, they turned homeward. The ear-splitting din of the caravan crawled away to the north.

For three decades those wooden wheels creaked

under a trade in peltry and pioneer commodities. Then
the railroads stretched their bright steel lines across the
north and the Red River carts were a conveyance of
the past. The oxen disappeared from the old trail with
the carts; and in the lumber camps and on the northern
farms they gave way, team by team, to horses. But their
work was not yet done in the great spaces. Their owners
sold them to westward moving immigrants; and so they
went on slowly to the sundown of their breed, hauling
the covered wagons of new settlers into the waiting
western country. Big strong patient beasts, laboring in
summer heat and winter cold, they broke the prairie sod
and dragged the crude go-devils through the wood. They
have their immortality in Babe, the great blue ox without whose mighty flanks and patient shoulders Paul Bunyan never could have come to fame.

The Red River trade on the Mississippi was an unexpected result of the planting of a famous Canadian
settlement by the Earl of Selkirk. In 1811 this Scotch
philantrophist, having secured a controlling interest in
the Hudson's Bay Company, acquired a vast tract of
land south and west of Lake Winnipeg. On this domain,
which he chose to call Assiniboia, he planned to settle
thousands of poverty-stricken peasants from Scotland.
When the colonists arrived in that remote country they
found their presence resented by the traders of the
North West Company, whose posts were already established in that region. That was the beginning of disappointment. Before many seasons they discovered that
their lot had been cast in an isolated and difficult land.
Cold, drought, grasshoppers, and mice made an accumu-

lation of hardships and discouragement. Finally two hundred and fifty of the colonists abandoned their claims and set out for the Mississippi, believing that the American authorities would give them land and farming outfits. Some of them squatted on the prairie near Fort Snelling, and so became the first civil residents of the upper valley. Others moved father down the Mississippi and settled in pioneer communities of Wisconsin and Illinois.

People left in the Red River country found their remote domain more productive of wild game than of farm crops. So their chief produce was peltry. Buffalo roamed the Pembina plains in such numbers that the Indians said they sprang like grass from the earth, and the streams were prodigal with beaver, fisher, otter, martin, and mink. The way to Fort Snelling on the Mississippi proved to be easier than the long trail to Hudson Bay, and so Fort Snelling, later St. Paul, became the great trading place for the Red River caravans. As their trade grew, Fort Snelling became a more important commerical point than Prairie du Chien, and it brought wealth to a trader at the pioneer settlement of Mendota, who became one of the striking and important figures in the Northwest.

Henry Hastings Sibley, who was to become the first governor of Minnesota, was born in Detroit of Massachusetts ancestry. From Detroit in the 1820's the first Lakes steamers were smoking their way to Mackinac and the border post of Sault Ste. Marie. In that direction young Henry Sibley's thoughts were drawn; he may have had a feeling that his future lay with the frontier. In 1828, at the age of seventeen, he went north, becoming a clerk in the sutler's store at Fort Brady beside the St. Mary's rapids at the foot of Lake Superior. There he learned to judge Indians and white men and to know the ways of trade in that country. Soon he was at Mackinac, the headquarters of the great American Fur Company, learning more about the business, growing more sure of himself, and hearing from the traders and the tribesmen the lore of the great country that lay to the north and the west. In 1834 Joseph Rolette and Hercules Dousman invited him to join them as a partner in operating a Mississippi outfit for the American Fur Company. By canoe and horseback he went to Mendota, near the head of navigation on the Mississippi. There at twenty-three years of age he became one of the important men in the fur trade. His post came to be the terminus for the long caravans of creaking carts from the Red River country.

Sibley exerted wide influence with both the traders and the Indians. He watched the commerce swell on the Mississippi, until the steamboats were disembarking hundreds of immigrants bound for the prairies of Minnesota and carrying away the fur cargoes brought to his warehouse by other hundreds of traders. At Mendota he built the first stone house in Minnesota, a symbol of the permanence of his life in that country. He foresaw clearly the commercial prospects of the region and he induced his wife's brother, Franklin Steele, to come north and have a part in it. At first Steele served as sutler at Fort Snelling. Soon he enlarged his interests, having an eye for prospective land values and the importance of water transport and water power. In time he became the pioneer lumberman on the Upper Mississippi.

Sibley's stone house at Mendota became famous for its hospitality. It was open alike to friends and strangers, and it was for many years a center of commercial, political, and cultural activities. Here were entertained such famous men as Joseph Nicollet, George Catlin, John Frémont, Stephen A. Douglas, as well as Indians from the Minnesota forests and half-breed drivers from the plains of Winnipeg. For these guests of the trade Sibley provided quarters on the upper floor, accessible by an outside stairway. They were free to come and go, and to stay beneath that generous roof for as long a time as they pleased.

Though he rose to eminence in the Northwest's civic and political life and kept abreast or ahead of the region's social evolution, Henry Sibley was always a man of the frontier. He led exploring parties into the northern forests and went on long hunting expeditions in the prairies of western Minnesota. These were strenuous and fruitful expeditions. In one winter hunt his party shot two thousand deer, fifty elk, fifty bears, and an uncounted number of buffalo. He was a trader who knew how to get peltry at its source as well as to bargain for it from the canoes of the Indians or the creaking carts of the Red River caravans.

CHAPTER 8

Western Fever

THE most villainously named among the Mississippi's tributaries is the Fever River. Found by the French in the fur-trading years, it was by right the *Fèbre* River, because its steep banks were softened with wild bean vines. But the French name gave way to a crudely phonetic English equivalent, and "Fever River" became the destination of thousands of fortune seekers who thronged to the lead mines in the 1830's. For a generation it poured a busy commerce into the Mississippi and its lead-veined valley became the first center of settlement north of St. Louis. In those years Fever River was a clear full stream, three hundred feet wide between its rugged shores, capable of carrying a commerce that made Galena, Illinois, the chief port of the West. Now it has shrunk to a shallow and uncertain creek, and only the most faithful maps show its course at all.

Lead was mined along Fever River long before the white man found that region. Radisson vaguely heard of lead diggings beyond the Winnebago country, and Tonty reported that the Indians were working lead mines near the Mississippi. The great trader Nicolas Perrot had more than a rumor of them; he was presented by a Miami chief with a chunk of lead which came from "the banks of a stream which empties into the Mississippi." Later Perrot was taken to the site and he taught the Indians how to cut the ore out from the rocks and melt it down to pure metal. From that time the production of lead became an adjunct to the fur trade, but as no quantity of heavy mineral could be carried in the voyageur's canoes its use was largely local.

A hundred years after Perrot's "discovery" Julien Dubuque came up the Mississippi to the lead district. He had great influence with the Indians and he easily persuaded the Fox tribe to grant him mineral rights on a creek that emptied into the west bank of the Mississippi. There for twenty years he produced lead in small but steady quantity. On his death in 1810 his shallow pits were abandoned.

It was not until the nineteenth century that American interests focused on the lead district. In 1816 that was a rough country, threaded by old Indian trails, known only to a few hunters and trappers. One of these trappers was Robert Grant, whose name now distinguishes the extreme southwestern county of Wisconsin, bordering on the Mississippi. Being habitually on the move, Grant had simplified his life by wearing his cooking kettle on his head under his coonskin cap. While tending his traps one day he was ambushed by a party of Indians. One of them hurled a tomahawk full force at his head. The kettle rang like a bell and the trapper stood unharmed. As the tomahawk fell to the ground the Indians fled in fright.

Robert Grant lived on among the old hacked hillsides where the lead cropped out. He was not a man to swing a pick in a breathless pocket or to sweat over a smelting fire. But the news spread and miners found their way to the dim forest trails beside the Fever River.

By 1826 the rush began and the lead district became the first intensive settlement above St. Louis.

Lead lay virtually on the surface of the ground. Some of the richest pockets began at the grass roots or were discovered by digging into gopher holes. Quickly there rose a dozen lawless communities, settlements like Hardscrabble and New Diggings, with the shallow pits honeycombing the hills around them. Any man with a pick and a shovel and a willing pair of shoulders could become a miner; the ore waited at his feet and ran in crooked veins along the ground. Even the subsurface veins could be worked without machinery; the ore was lifted out in buckets on a hand windlass. After smelting in open-air ovens it was run into molds and it came out "pig lead" ready for market.

Some of the settlers dug relatively deep mines and worked them the year round. They lived in tents during the summer and in winter they took to the abandoned shafts that slanted into the hillsides. Other miners came to the diggings with the warm sun of spring and in the fall drove back with wagonloads of ore to the Illinois settlements. It was not many seasons before distinguishing names were attached to the two varieties of miners: the year-round residents who wintered in the hillsides became "Badgers," and those who swarmed south in autumn were named "Suckers" for a fish that runs south in the western rivers during the autumn months. So Wisconsin and Illinois received their nicknames from the pioneer miners of lead.

Hardscrabble and New Diggings were primitive camps, but in the thirties the lead district boasted the sizable and permanent towns of Galena, Platteville,

Dodgeville, Wiota, and Mineral Point. Wiota was orig-
Inally named Hamilton's Diggings for William S. Hamilton, the son of Alexander Hamilton, who was early
taken with the western fever. He became an important
figure in the new region. Platteville had its famous "Grocery Street," which was lined with groggeries, and no
woman ever ventured into that part of the settlement.
The town itself was pitted with diggings, some only
grave-deep, others as deep as a well. It was perilous for
a man to stagger away from Grocery Street with those
pitfalls awaiting him. Many a Platteville miner, and occasionally a cow or a pig browsing in the night, bawled
for help from the bottom of a played-out shaft.

Mineral Point, the commercial center of the upper
lead mines, was originally named Shake Rag. In the
early 1830's a stream of Cornish miners came up the
Fever River to add their variety to the motley population of the district. They had left the depleted tin mines
of Cornwall, and they were true Badgers who arrived
in the Fever River valley to stay. So they built stone
houses out of native limestone blocks a foot thick, erecting them in a neat row on one side of the hill, with their
mines on the slope opposite. At mealtime the women
stood in their doorways and waved a sheet or a cloth as a
signal that food was on the table, and from that practice their settlement became Shake Rag. Within a few
years Mineral Point grew to the proportions of a small
metropolis with half a dozen nationalities represented
among its citizens. But it retains its original name in
Shake Rag Street, which runs along the hillside and is
still lined with the solid stone cottages built a century
ago.

As the mines reached their height of production in the early forties, the road from Dodgeville through Mineral Point to Galena (now U. S. 151) became the most busy and vital highway on the frontier. A motley and endless traffic stirred up the summer dust, slogged through the mud of spring and autumn, and toiled over the frozen ruts of winter. All the strains of frontier life were there—homesteaders seeking new country, speculators bent on sudden wealth, miners with a scanty grubstake and an ardent hope, pioneer preachers carrying the gospel into lawless country. Families of Swiss farmers discouraged by the hardships of their bleak fields in the Selkirk colony came down the Mississippi to the busy lead diggings. Irish immigrants and gnarled little Cornishmen, at home in the ground like moles, sank their shafts into the hillsides. A Missourian named Henry Dodge came north with his colony of slaves, promising them freedom if they would work the mines for a season. He took out three thousand dollars' worth of ore in his first winter, and later became territorial governor of Wisconsin. Along with new people came herds of cattle and droves of hogs, lumber wagons and loads of machinery for the smelters and the mines, stagecoaches and heavy freighting wagons. Amid this noisy traffic the laden ore wagons creaked on their way to Galena.

Inevitably Galena, at the head of navigation on the Fever River, became the commercial depot of the district. Steamboat captains were induced to risk the rapids of the Mississippi to carry the lead trade and Galena became the principal port above St. Louis. In and out of Galena the ox teams plodded and the wagons swayed on the rutted roads. The Yankee drivers, patient men, sure of themselves, with the set lines of Maine and Massachusetts in their faces, drove quietly, using a good stick. But more of the ore wagons were in the hands of western drivers, men who drove with their voices, hurling a flood of curses over the broad backs of their teams. Legend said that an ox couldn't stand to be taken from a Grant County man and hitched to a Yankee's wagon. Accustomed to a Westerner's roaring, his spirit was broken by silence.

Galena in the boom years was a busy, boisterous town jammed between rocky hills, with houses which an eastern visitor compared to a flock of sheep going down to water. Nearly every person in town could stand on his own front step and look down on the river where the steamboats churned in to the landing. When the long lines of ore wagons creaked through the streets and the steamers daily disgorged hundreds of new families eager to stake their claims in the district, Galena was vibrant with frontier energy and expectation. Thousands of people coming up the Fever River found a spirit unlike that of older regions of America. Here was the free, unbounded country, the new land teeming with life and bright with promise. In the 1840's Galena was a rival of Chicago, with a prospect of becoming the great metropolis of the Middle West. There was, after all, a fever in that valley. It was the Western Fever.

Like a fever it burned itself out. The peak of lead production came in 1847 and a long period of decline began. The restless people moved on, to the mines of the Far West and the rich prairie farms across the Mississippi. The patient ones stayed, like the slaves of Governor Dodge whose descendants still live in the region

around Dodgeville. The miners turned to farming and
the lead district became a dairy country with fine herds
of cattle browsing over pastures pocked and pitted with
forgotten diggings.

The noisy towns settled down to a quiet and
dwindling life, and the Fever River, after the timber was
cut from the coulees and the marshes were drained for
farm land, dwindled to a shallow, mud-filled stream.
When in 1855 the railroad pushed on past Galena to the
Mississippi, Galena became a way station. When steamers could no longer ascend to the deserted Fever River
landings, it gave up dreams of greatness and was overshadowed by younger cities—Moline, Davenport, Keokuk, Rock Island. Finally, to taunt the town that had
had its brief period of drama and its feverish era of trade,
the Dubuque city council proposed a resolution that the
bed of Fever River be plowed up and planted to potatoes.

But history had one more dealing with Galena. In
the spring of 1861 in the sleepy Fever River town, a
blunt, slow, bearded man, looking more than his thirty-
eight years, was stacking hides in his father's tannery.
Already he had been cashiered from the army and had
made a fiasco of business and farming; people said there
was a smell of failure about him. Four years later he was
meeting Robert E. Lee in the farmhouse at Appomattox. When he had won the Union victory, people at
Galena began to remember his massive face and his
massive movements. He had said, "I will fight it out on
this line if it takes all summer." That was the way they
remembered him, stubborn and slow and blinking a

little, like a bear just come out of a cave. He was a man slow as time to take hold of a thing, but slow as all eternity to let it go. Anyway, shabby Cap Grant of Galena was a world figure at the end.

CHAPTER 9

The Saga of Cleng Peerson

ON a summer evening in 1833, while the heat of an August sun still lay over the level plains of Illinois, a lonely figure moved across the land, facing the sunset and the Mississippi, the great river that waited somewhere in the west. He was a small man in clothing that smelled of dust and of campfires, and he carried a faded blue sack slung over his shoulder. Weariness showed plainly in his steps and something more than fatigue was in his face; even his light-blue eyes had lost their quickness. He trudged ahead with his gaze on the ground and his shapeless hat pulled down to shield him from the sunset flame. But in spite of fatigue his legs swung through the prairie grass with that free stride which is the mark of wanderers the world over. One could tell this man from a tiller of the soil.

He had reason to be weary. He had walked fifteen hundred miles from the shores of Lake Ontario through broad Ohio counties green with June, across the low fields of Michigan, and past the little lakes of Indiana. At Chicago, a cluster of stilted huts in a marsh, he had turned north, for five days tramping at the water's edge, printing his steps in the blank sands of Lake Michigan. A windy blue world and a white surf were grateful to him after weeks of encircling prairie—this man had been a sailor in his youth. At night he made a fire of sticks at the lake's edge, boiling his pot of tea, and he slept under starlight and the soothing drone of water.

At the site of Milwaukee (three log houses—one of them empty) he found a tall, dark, handsome, bearded man, naked from the waist, standing beside his cabin with rows of traps hanging from wooden pegs and freshly webbed snowshoes drying in the sun. This was Solomon Juneau, fur trader, a man of the deep woods and the secret waters, looking half Indian in his fringed trousers and beaded moccasins. There was a pungent odor of peltry all about the place.

The traveler peered at him shrewdly and spoke in French. "What will I find if I continue north from here?"

"Nothing but woods, to the world's end," was the reply.

"And what in this direction?" He pointed inland.

"Prairie, and at last the great river."

Satisfied, the small man turned back, striding southwest over the level country, keeping his eyes open, searching the land like a hunter. Day after day he tramped through rolling grasslands, occasionally crossing a wooded ridge or swimming a clear stream that flowed west toward the great river. Nights he spent on the starlit prairie, his dying campfire the only sign of man in all that country. He found no roads and no habitation, not even a wigwam. Then, after a few days, the ridges were gone and he was in a flat and dreary land that had no ending. The horizon retreated; he seemed to walk a treadmill. The scorching prairie sun found him and followed him day after day. His skin burned brown like an Indian's. The food in his sack ran low and he grew weak from fatigue and hunger. But still he walked on because that was his business and because there was nothing else to do.

Now, at the end of an August day, he was tired in body and in mind. The long hot plain was printed on his sun-spent eyes, and like a great and weary blankness it oppressed his memory. But all at once, as the sunset ebbed across the empty land, he sensed a difference. His tired stride quickened and his eyes swept ahead to a grassy hill. When he stood on that rise dusk was falling, but the blue twilight showed a large and gently sloping meadow within the wide curve of a river fringed with oak and willow trees whose crowns held the last warm light of day. Unconsciously the man had bared his head. After a long, circling gaze he threw himself on the grass, and thanked God for guiding his steps to such a land. Then, weak as he was from heat and hunger and fatigue, he fell asleep.

While he slept he dreamed of the broad prairie meadow by the quiet river; but it was no longer an empty pasture of wild pea vines and buffalo grass. He saw fine fields, crisscrossed with rows of ribboned corn and green with wheat and barley, and fenced pastures where fat cattle grazed, their udders swelled with milk. Between the fields ran straight white roads, joining one farm to another. The barns and stables were painted red, with white bargeboards and white window sills. The houses were white, gleaming like frost when the sun was on them; each one had a many-colored garden before it and a flagstaff rising from the garden with a flag high over all. In the very center of the prairie was a steep-roofed church with a bell showing in the airy

tower. The windows were open to the summer sun, and on the breeze was borne very clearly an old stately hymn sung in the churches of Norway.

When the little man awoke he felt curiously restored. It was morning, cool and fresh, with an eastern light slanting across the plain. While he boiled his tea over a fire of twisted fagots of grass he looked more closely at the land. Yes, there were broad acres lush with wild pea vines and prairie grass. There were thickets of trees, creeks, a richly wooded river flowing westward toward the Mississippi. He dug into the prairie with the long blade of his clasp knife. Beneath the matted grass roots he uncovered a fine black soil that crumbled quickly in his fingers.

That autumn he walked back to Lake Ontario. In the following summer he led the first Norwegian colony into the Mississippi basin and established the Fox River settlement in northern Illinois. The dream was beginning to come true. Cleng Peerson was the name of this strange, Norse pioneer; and his story is a part of the great wonder tale of America.

2

He was born Klein Pederson, on a hill farm called Hesthammer, a few miles north of Stavanger, Norway; but he tried various spellings with his name. A sailor in his youth, then a tradesman, a friend of the Quakers, perhaps a dissenter from the state church, finally a pathfinder in America and for thirty years a colonizer and a follower of the frontier, Cleng Peerson became a legend in himself.

In the Scandinavian settlements of Minnesota, people who never saw Cleng Peerson told each other how he always carried in his pocket a silver shilling, which for years he offered for entertainment on his travels; but no one ever took the money, and that was his only property. He never worked for gain, but always for other people. Standing on the river landings in Wisconsin, men remembered that Cleng Peerson had traveled up and down the great valley, in steamboats and in oxcarts, but mostly on foot before there was any other way. He had been a carpenter in the old country, but in America he plied no trade. He wandered over the land with his blue eyes always roving; when he stopped at a settlement he lived at ease, paying for his keep with shrewd advice and those droll stories that were the fruit of wandering; and all too soon he was gone again.

"He was not a man that worked," they would say if anyone asked his trade.

"Hard work," they explained, "was never to his liking."

In a Dakota farmhouse on a winter evening, the children asked for a story. "And how would you like a Cleng Peerson story? Well—*Cleng Peerson traveled on foot through the States fifty years ago and founded six and thirty settlements. One day he was sitting under a tree where Chicago now stands, and a half-breed came up and offered to sell him one hundred acres of land on that very spot, if only he would change clothes with him, and give him his pipe. But Cleng hesitated. He was a cleanly chap; he was afraid there might be lodgers in the other man's clothes. That property today is worth more than the whole of the national revenue of Norway!"*

It is true, Cleng Peerson hadn't a view to money; he never got rich. A smart man who spoke English fluently and knew enough of other languages to make himself understood with Germans and Frenchmen, he found thousands of acres for his folk to settle but he never owned a rod of land himself. Sometimes at an odd task that pleased his fancy he picked up a few dollars, which he quickly gave away to the needy. The women told each other how, when he had no money, he would beg from the rich and give to the poor. They had their own fond stories about him. It was true that he was a vagabond who had left a wife somewhere across the water; but, they liked to say, "Was ever a man so good to children?" And what a great talker, "with more tales than you could ever remember!" And "see him now with his arms always out for the orphans! . . . Who hasn't seen him carrying children on his back for miles to find good homes for them?"

Something of the child and something of the troll was in him, flashing in his impish smile and the light that danced in his eyes. He would stand and knock at the open door of a woman's house, with that look on his face, his head hanging a little on one side, his cap crushed in his hand, and his sunburned hair all rumpled on his forehead. Inside, he would ask her to make coffee. Then he would take the knitting from her basket and lie down on the bed and knit and tell a wonder tale of his travels while the coffee brewed. He might be just back from Norway, or he had toured the scattered settlements. He was as good as a long letter telling about people one knew, carrying messages between friends. He made the heart kindle and loosed the mind to travel at his heels; and the best in the humble larder was not too good for such a man.

Cleng Peerson came and went over the sea as well as over the prairie. Picture him now in 1842 in the tavern of a steep little Norwegian town clad in a long coat and a fur cap, telling a circle of excited listeners about the glories of America. He speaks a broken Norwegian-English, for in America there are things that have no Old World names. His thin little face is full of ardor, the eager light of his blue eyes flashes back and forth over the group and he seems to be speaking to each man personally. Listening, the Norwegian villagers forget the snow blowing outside the tavern door, the candles guttering in the draft, and the dark rafters of the room; they are seeing that country of wide horizons and forest-lined rivers where the rich land is waiting for the plow. Even the tavernkeeper is leaning on the counter with distance in his eyes, so that a stranger seeking food has to tug at the man's apron.

They had many questions to ask him, and he was ready with the answers. Cleng Peerson was at his best in a crowd. He could be very persuasive. And when they were silent again, he went on to tell what a man could expect in America. Bread and pork and milk always on his table. A farm of two hundred *tonderland,*—two hundred, mind you,—not a patch of ground such as the crofters tilled, fit only for a garden in America; and all that land to be had for the taking! And in America there were other things to wonder at. For instance, a poor man who worked hard and hadn't any too much

for his needs, didn't need to take his hat off to the parson, or the magistrate, or even the President of the
United States himself! He was as good as anybody and
he had every chance to show what was in him.

Long after they had left the tavern the crofters sat
up at home, their strong faces thoughtful, their slow
minds going over what Cleng Peerson had said. There
was not much chance for them in the old country. The
soil was poor and most of the land was up and down
anyway, mountainsides not fit for farming. But in
America! A man could hardly believe what big farms
they had there, debt-free and with soil so deep you could
never get to the bottom of it. And no high taxes, no
military service to take a young man's strength from his
acres. Perhaps in time a crofter might have a big *gaard*
for himself, yes, a big farm all his own and a white house
with a scrollwork on the gables, and a barnyard with his
own sheds and stables. "Cleng Peerson said so." That
was enough! This light-footed fellow didn't look like
a leader, or a builder, but folk said that there was a mag-
net in his pocket: Wherever he went he drew men after
him—from Lake Ontario to Fox River, from Fox River
to the Mississippi, from the Mississippi to the Trinity and
Brazos rivers in faraway Texas. He was a man always
seeking rivers.

Nobody ever knew why Cleng Peerson came to
America, to begin with. There was a vague story about
his marriage to a wealthy elderly widow in the old
country, and about his difficulties with her which may
have put into his head the idea of clearing out and seeing
what America was like. At any rate, he came in 1821,
before there was a Norsky anywhere in all the States,

he and his friend, Knud Olsen Eide; but Knud fell sick and died in New York City, and then Cleng was alone. For three years he tramped about the country on foot, becoming accustomed to the strangeness of America, examining soils, observing American methods of agriculture, learning manners and laws and languages. A trip to Norway in 1824 gave him opportunity to report his findings to the Quakers, and they followed him back across the water in the next year. These were the "Sloopers," the party of fifty souls from Stavanger, the first of that great host who left the woods and slopes above the Baltic and the hard toil and grinding poverty of the homeland, to seek their fortunes in America.

3

It was a long way and weeks of gray Atlantic from the blue cliffs of Norway to the uncertain shores of America. Behind, like a weight pulling at the heart, the homeland was fading; each day it lay farther off and harder to recover, and each day the sweetness and sadness were heavier to bear.

Things came back now with a clearness and a closeness: they blended in simple, old designs that showed life secure and lighted by such joys as poor men might know. After rain in the valleys the air smelled of juniper and leaves and heather, and in the evening the young folk lighted bonfires on the hills and sang their songs together. At the lonely *saeters* there was the serenity of sheep browsing over the uplands in the long June twilight. On winter evenings the fire was rosy on the stones and hands were busy, a woman spinning at her wheel, a man binding brooms of birch twigs for the market. It was strange how much hurt could lie in the memory of little things.

Driven below decks by wind and rain, the men leaned on their elbows across the table talking long and earnestly about America.

"They say a man can make four Norwegian dollars a day, working on the canal with a shovel."

"Four dollars? And who said that?"

"Cleng Peerson himself. I heard him say it at the Elvedalen tavern. With my own ears I heard him say that."

"Four dollars!" They remembered how a woman could go out baking, making other people's bannocks for six cents a day, and how the crofters did their statutory work at the pay of eight cents and a meal of rice, and a man could saw wood all day for twelve cents and be glad to get that.

There were other strange things in America.

"You know a man has got to have a new name over there."

"Why is that so?"

"So he can file his papers to claim his land."

"Can't a man claim his land by the name of Larsen?"

"Well, you see there are many Larsens. If twenty men claimed land in the name of Lars Larsen, there would be trouble. They couldn't keep them separate."

"Twenty Lars Larsens taking up land? Yes! A man wouldn't know, himself, which was his land!"

"Yes," and the heads nodded earnestly. "Yes. Of course. That's bad. All those Lars Larsens wouldn't do in America. But where can a man find a new name to go by?"

"That's not so hard. He can take the name of his town or the farm he comes from. Why there's Hans Hansen, you know what name he goes by in America?"

"No. I thought he was still Hans Hansen."

"No. He has a new name. In America he's Hans Gilderhaus."

"Hans Gilderhaus. That's a fine name to go by. Hans Gilderhaus."

"That's the way we'll find it in America." There is a boast in the faces now and somebody says:

"Tune up the fiddle, Tellef."

Down by the end of the bench sits an old crofter in a sheepskin cap, with a red comforter about his neck. He is tearing a tobacco plug to pieces with his dark-stained fingers to fill his pipe. Some of the strongest men can't smoke on this trip, they put their pipes away when their stomachs begin to churn; but this old man fished for many seasons off Lofoten.

" 'Oleana'!" somebody demands. " 'Oleana'! Tellef, 'Oleana'!"

Carefully, the old man lays his pipe on the mess table, tamping the ash down in the bowl with his forefinger to keep the coal on it. He puts the fiddle to his chin and twangs it sharply. Their voices pick up the noisy song:

In America they give you land for nothing,
And the grain just pops out of the ground. Golly, that's
easy!
        Ole—Ole—Ole—Oh! Oleana!
        Ole—Ole—Ole—Oh! Oleana!

The grain threshes itself in the granary,
  While I stretch out at ease in my bunk.

And the crops, you just ought to see the potatoes!
  You can distill a quart of whisky out of each one of them.

The salmon leap like mad in the rivers,
  And hop into the kettles and cry out for a cover.

And little roast pigs rush about the streets,
  Politely inquiring if you wish for ham.

And the hens lay eggs as big as a gourd,
  And the cocks strike the hour like an eight-day clock.

You bet, they give you two dollars a day for carousing,
  And if you are good and lazy, they'll probably give you
    four.

And we stalk about the streets with velvet coats and silver
    buttons,
  Smoking meerschaum pipes which the old woman fills
    for us.

Oh, I'd much rather live in America
  Than drag the chains of slavery over there in Norway.

           Ole—Ole—Ole—Oh! Oleana!
           Ole—Ole—Ole—Oh! Oleana!

      Yes, it is a fine country, America! But at the far
end of the table, sitting alone, is another old man,
stooped and gray and lean as a crow, wearing leaden
rings in his ears. He knows a song full of homesickness
and heart pull:

Farewell, Norway, and God bless thee,
  Stern and severe wert thou always,
But as a mother I honor thee,
  Even though thou has skimped my bread.
All things vanish;
  Grief and care sink down upon the heart.
Still the memory of thee refreshes the soul
  Like the deep sleep of a child. . . .
Night has fallen. . . .
  Oh, God, let not the ties break
  That bind me to the North.

This is not the longing for an easy land.

Despite the rollicking stanzas of "Oleana," these exiles know that loneliness and toil await them in America. They have heard the pathfinders, who came back with praise for America, but with warning too. They know the fate of Ole Rynning, a clergyman's son and a scholar of the University of Christiania, who found defeat and death in the New Canaan. When the gloom envelops them they tell the story: how Ole Rynning wandered the wintry swamps of Illinois and, at last, staggered on his torn and frozen feet into the Beaver Creek settlement: how, as he lay dying in a sod house, with the icy wind piercing him through chinks in the walls, he wrote the thirteen chapters of his *True Account of America*. Somewhere on that vast prairie of their hopes the body of Ole Rynning lies under the soil. A strong and a good man, a scholar, a leader. Yet Ole Rynning did not wish to discourage anyone from going to America although he told the whole, the true story, writing down everything he had time for, with death coming always closer each day. Some of them might perish, like

Ole and others he wrote about. Still no one of them could foresee what would happen to him; so, for every one of them there was hope. They felt that they already knew something of hardship. All their lives they had been trying to turn little patches among the rocks into grainfields, they had caried sacks of earth on their backs to spread in places where the hoe rang on the bedrock underneath. Now there was a dream in their minds, a dream of deep soil.

4

It was these people whom Cleng Peerson led to the fertile river valley in Illinois. And from Fox River he led them west again, to the Mississippi itself and across it to the wild lands of the territories. Patiently, with hope and resolution, the big Norsemen plodded at his side: Jacob and Knud Slogvig, and Sjur Haakin; Peter and William Testman; Ansten Nattestad, Halvor Knudson, Ole Kjolvik; and many others at various times. They moved in the old Scandinavian fashion: not individually nor in families, but in groups and colonies of a hundred or so. They strengthened each other.

There was a story that when Cleng visited Bishop Hill, the Swedish colony in Illinois, in 1847, he got married there. Lars Tallakson, who had wandered away from the colony, said so, insisting that he had lent Cleng his own hat for the wedding. But that was a likely tale. Certainly Cleng Peerson never stopped his wandering, and in all his stories about himself he never let on having a wife in America. He saw thousands of homes set up for others while he had not so much as a lean-to for himself. He lived like a tramp for thirty years.

At the end of that time, when the pathfinder led his last slow caravan, southward this time, to the sunny plains of Bosque County, Texas, where he died, the prairie settlements were growing strong and many. At Fox River, the mother of them all, more than two hundred families were farming the rich valley where the little man had dreamed; and from that colony many laden oxcarts had creaked away to begin new settlements in the oak openings of Wisconsin and the territories across the Mississippi. Before they had learned even a few tags of English they had been caught by the westward pull.

The largest and most prosperous of these Norse settlements in Wisconsin was Koshkonong, with its two board churches among the huts and cabins of five hundred families from Telemarken, Voss, and Numedal. Muskego, despite the marshes along the lake shore, attracted three hundred settlers from Numedal, Hallingdal, and Land; and here was the house of that famous gentleman and innkeeper, Even Heg, who welcomed so many newcomers to the wilderness and sent them on with friendly counsel and shrewd advice. Even Heg set up a printing press in his barn in 1847 and established the first Norwegian-American newspaper, *Nordlyset*. The first issue contained a complete translation of the Declaration of Independence. Here, to Muskego, Lars Rekve, who had worked for a year on a Lake Michigan steamer, brought Nils and Ole Gilderhaus. They stopped for a while with Thorstein Bjaadland, a cobbler, who mended their shoes while they sat smoking their pipes

in his hut. Then, well fed and freshly shod, they set out
north to found a settlement of their own.

The Norwegians came first; in their wake followed
Danes, Swedes, Icelanders. The Danes founded a colony
on Washington Island in Green Bay; the Swedes raised
New Upsala beside the waters of the Wisconsin River.
The Norskies came always in growing numbers. Jefferson Prairie filled up with Sognings and Vossings, and
Rock Prairie prospered with its two hundred families
from Numedal and Hallingdal. Beaver Creek, Scoponing, Pine Lake, Ashippun, Heart Prairie—there were
no roads to these settlements, only wagon tracks along
the section lines. But the oxcarts found the way and a
tide of migration groped across the land, a tide that was
to sweep on for half a century through unmapped miles
of forest and across other miles of meadows and little
ridged hills, until at last it broke over the far leagues
of the Dakotas and the plains of Saskatchewan.

For the Norse people came to the North. They
could not have settled in Carolina, or New Mexico, any
more than the long-necked loon with its cold cry and
its thick northern plumage could live in Louisiana
bayous. Cleng Peerson looked for their land, and though
he spent thirty years following the watercourses—the
Mohawk, Fox, and Salt rivers, Sugar Creek, the mighty-
flowing Mississippi, and lastly the Brazos, Trinity, and
Sabine of the south—he didn't find it. He took his last
turn to Texas; but the anonymous men were already
scanning the vast buffalo ranges beyond the Mississippi.
One man, even a pathfinder, can be led astray. The folk
have another wisdom; and, though their choices seem the

fruit of accident and chance, time reveals the pattern. One bird's flight is voluntary, capricious, and free; when the flock is migrant there is another force and another beauty, inseparable from instinct and need.

Tish-ah! said the grass . . . Tish-ah, Tish-ah! . . . Never had it said anything else—never would it say anything else. But in time the voices from Trondhjem and Upsala, from Helsingfors and Copenhagen were heard in the shadow of the pineries and under the tall blue prairie sky. Something led them, not Cleng Peerson or any man; something more impersonal and significant, a destiny and the nature of a people. So they came to the North, a folk who could face loneliness and winter's cold and the uncertainty of harvest for the peculiar glory of the soil, who had a brooding mind and an enduring nature, like the ice-locked land and the rock-rooted forest that gave birth to their river, the Mississippi.

CHAPTER 10

From Helsingland to Bishop Hill

In Sweden the district of Helsingland was rich in iron, timber, and flax; and full of thrifty industrious peasants who held their own land in fee simple. In those broad meadows and shelving forests there was no system of great landed estates such as dominated the provinces below Stockholm and Karlstad. The independent farmers raised rice, flax, and potatoes and lived in neat red-painted farmhouses surrounded by patches of bright flowers in orderly garden plots. Fine roads crossed the meadows and led to prosperous market towns. At the beginning of the nineteenth century it seemed that nothing could disrupt the systematic life of this province, and there was no reason to picture hundreds of peasant families breaking prairie sod in the distant valley of the Mississippi. But then came Eric Jansen.

Eric Jansen was a farm boy like any number of other lads in the fertile province of Helsingland. But with a difference. He had a genius for religious revelation. Born in Biskopskulla parish, Uppland, he spent a boyhood of much toil and little learning and developed a miraculous power of will. As a young man he suffered from extreme rheumatic pains, but would not submit to them. A particularly severe attack, which overtook him while he plowed his father's flax field, left him unconscious in the furrow. As he returned to consciousness, opening his eyes to the blue Swedish sky, he heard a voice speak more plainly than any he had ever heard from human lips: *All things are possible to him that believeth. . . . If ye ask anything in my name, I will do it, saith the Lord.* Young Eric Jansen, rising to his knees, asked for health. At the moment his pain left him, never to return.

The want of faith in those about him oppressed Eric Jansen from this time on. He became a lay preacher, tramping the roads and moors of Osterunda parish with a worn Bible under his arm, letting his feet find the way while his pale eyes scanned the open page of Scripture. When he began to oppose Lutheran doctrines, setting the Bible above all devotional literature, pleading for the inner faith instead of the outward forms of piety elevated by the established church, his preaching aroused opposition. With opposition his convictions grew. He had matchless powers of debate and he knew his Bible, book, chapter, and verse: he was ready for controversy with the clergy.

Controversy was not strong enough to combat Swedish pietism, though it made foes for the young zealot. When he showed himself impervious to verbal attack, Eric Jansen began to suffer violence. His meetings were dispersed, the houses of his associates were stoned, his followers were assaulted. But they praised God for their persecution and stood in front of parsonages and prayed in loud voices for the salvation of the pastors. They marched on the highways at evening singing hymns, their voices drifting over the dusky fields and moving people strangely; at midnight they gathered in woods and hills, and from their dim conventicles rose rumors of a new kind of peasant insurrection. Yet their doctrine was simple and harmless—"Godliness with a contented mind is winning enough."

But Eric Jansen was not so simple; he was wondered at and feared.

There was nothing fearful about him, but there was a mystery in the power he wielded over others. A man of medium stature, he had smoke-blue eyes, a pale three-cornered face with thin lips, prominent teeth, and high cheekbones. His voice was harsh and indistinct, he spoke as though his mouth were filled. He preached in the manner of the Wesleyans, his voice rising and trembling with great fervor. Often he wept streaming tears in the midst of prayer or sermon; always he wore a strained and terrible grin, the result of a muscular contraction. At the height of eloquence he threw up his right hand with its index finger missing: that finger had been chopped off by his brother with an ax in their father's wood lot. And in certain moods he had an hypnotic eye which fastened itself with a strange intensity, and commanded. Years later, during the terrible season of cholera on the bleak Illinois plain, many of his followers stricken with disease asked his blessing. "Go and die in peace," Eric Jansen said, and they dragged themselves alone over the prairie, contented with their fate.

From those first years of preaching in Sweden, Eric Jansen showed himself a master of men. Inevitably the magistrates and the churchmen thought him dangerous. Tried before the court of Westerås for publicly burning the works of Luther, Arnd, and Nohrberg, he was released and went in triumph preaching to great crowds out of doors while the churches stood empty. Those left unmoved by his preaching were converted by the touch of that outstretched hand with the index finger missing. In a new fit of zeal he held a public burning of the hymnbook and the catechism; only the Bible was divine. The persecution grew. Six times he was arrested; his followers were fined. At last a price was put on Eric Jansen's head, and he was hunted like a wolf.

When he was captured his followers took him by violence from the crown official and carried him over the mountains to Norway. There, hiding for his life, he thought out his theology. He, Eric Jansen, was appointed to restore the true Christianity which had been extinct since the time of Constantine and the end of the persecutions. He, Eric Jansen, represented the second coming of Christ. He, Eric Jansen, was to separate the children of God from the worldlings and gather them together. At this stage he saw destiny pointing to America. Freedom and holiness found no home in Sweden, corrupted with prejudice and error. The New World was the refuge for the sanctified. In America he would build the New Jerusalem. Immediately he sent out the call to his followers. Without hesitation they sold their property in Sweden and contributed their means to the common fund.

In the prairie heat of July, 1846, Eric Jansen led four hundred of his followers west from Chicago to their lonely settlement, in the present Henry County, Illinois. To a little river near a great river in the New World they came, and not without hardship and disaster. Within a few seasons eleven hundred of them had come, in a dozen ships. One vessel of that number was lost at sea and there were no survivors. Another was

wrecked on the rocks of Newfoundland, a third was five
months on the way. From New York to Buffalo they had
journeyed by river and canal, then by three lakes to
Chicago, where Eric Jansen met every new detachment
of the faithful. At Chicago they bought horses and
wagons for the invalids and the baggage; the rest set
out on foot over the level land. Ten days and nights on
the prairie with faces turned to the west, and steps seem-
ing small in that great loneliness, following the little
streams that led toward the west. A long column it was,
moving slowly through the buffalo grass with Eric Jansen at the head, like Moses—an Old Testament picture
of the wandering tribes in the wilderness seeking the
Promised Land.

For their town, which in a surprising mood of
reminiscence he named Bishop Hill for his native parish,
Eric Jansen chose a rise of land shaded with oak trees
and commanding miles of unbroken prairie. To house
them for the winter the colonists built log cabins, sod
houses, and dugouts in the wall of the ravine where Edwards Creek flowed toward the Mississippi. These were
products of haste and inexperience. Before the winter
was over the dark cramped dwellings took a drastic toll
of life. In one dugout for unmarried women were three
tiers of beds and three occupants in each bed, fifty-two
women altogether. With the raw wet earth for floor,
roof, and wall, dampness and cold were constant bed-
fellows. Soon ague set in. Many mornings a fresh corpse
was carried from that dim cave to a smaller and more
lonely one a mile across the prairie.

Along with those first buildings, a great tabernacle,
shaped in the form of a cross, had been erected of logs

and canvas. It held a thousand worshipers. Eric Jansen himself roused the folk at five each morning for devotions. Often he prayed for two unbroken hours. A similar service closed the day; there were three on Sundays. In the summer growing season the only service was a midday open-air session in the grove. At all times, with evangelical zeal, the brethren prayed for the salvation of others. Twelve young men were elected to systematize Jansen theology and prepare it for missionary dispersion. In due time they set forth to the four corners of America, carrying the word.

During the first year the colonists broke three hundred and fifty acres of prairie and set up three and one-half miles of sod fence. They built gristmills and sawmills and learned to manufacture kiln-dried bricks. Remembering their Swedish arts, they grew flax and made linen. Their woven products went to a dozen towns on the Ohio and the Mississippi, finding ready sale at good prices. Resourceful to try new crops, and new methods of harvesting them, the settlers planted a plot in broomcorn and sold the yield as far away as Boston. They reaped their first grain harvest in the familiar Swedish style with scythes and rakes. The second year they used the improved cradle. To secure the grain against bad weather they worked the cradles day and night until the men weakened. Then they decided that eighteen hours should constitute a day's work. Young men swung the cradles, middle-aged men and women bound the sheaves, children gathered them together, old men set them up in shocks. The third season they used a reaper and did the work in half the time. That fall they hired a threshing machine to winnow

their grain and, having studied it carefully, built a better machine for themselves.

Bishop Hill was a true commune. The members enjoyed equal division of labor, work for men, work for women, work for children over fourteen years; and a sharing of all the colony's produce. They ate their meals as one family in a dining hall two hundred feet long; they sang hymns (for Eric Jansen, having burned the Lutheran hymnbook and catechism in those last harried months in Sweden, had now compiled them anew) and carried on their toil together. When the harvest was ended, men, women, and children marched through the yellow fields, hands joined and faces lighted, singing merry folk songs. The march ended with a harvest feast in the great dining hall and a fervent period of preaching and prayer.

In 1850 Bishop Hill was prosperous and growing. Eleven hundred people lived in industrious harmony, fourteen hundred acres of prairie were under cultivation. The colonists had put fifteen thousand gold dollars into circulation in Henry County where trade had been only by barter in terms of mink and beaver skins, and they were sending back letters to every part of Sweden, preparing for the great tide of Swedish emigration to America. Over this strong commonwealth Eric Jansen, with his pale and burning eyes and the weasel-grin on his sharp face, was spiritual and temporal ruler. He preached and prayed, bought and sold, appointed agents and representatives and carried on the colony's growing business in the towns along the Mississippi from St. Louis to La Crosse.

Then came fate in the person of John Root, wan-

derer and adventurer. In autumn when the hickories
were barred with yellow and all the oaks were bronzed,
he came walking over the prairie in buckskin clothing
with a knife in his belt and a long rifle on his shoulder.
The son of a Swedish gentleman, he was a man of pleasing manner and adventurous life. He had been serving
in the United States Army in the Mexican campaigns
and, on his discharge, he set out for Bishop Hill. He soon
made it apparent that he had no taste for prayer or earnest labor. He spent his time hunting and roving. When
he sat on the benches in the dining hall and talked of his
wanderings on land and sea there was an uneasy sac-
rilege in the faces of the children of God. One of his rapt
listeners was the niece of Eric Jansen. A quiet girl with
eyes strangely shy and lovely, she found her heart beating against her woolsey tunic when the newcomer's gaze
followed her. Before long, for John Root was a forth-
right man, she was his wife. But even his lovely bride
could not make Bishop Hill other than a tame place for
the soldier of fortune. Soon John Root went roving
again, as guide and interpreter for a Jewish peddler who
passed that way. The peddler was seen no more; later,
the decayed body of a murdered man was found under
the floor of a deserted cabin sixty miles across the prairie.
After four months' absence, John Root returned alone
to Bishop Hill. Eric Jansen tried to separate his wife
from him and there was wrath between them. One day
John Root came in from target practice and shot Eric
Jansen dead.

Eric Jansen's successor as ruler of the colony was
his wife, a remarkable woman who had now outlived
four husbands: a drowned seaman, a schoolmaster who

had followed her from Sweden to Illinois and died on the prairie with a broken heart when she refused to leave the Jansenites, a devout Bishop Hill farmer, and finally Eric Jansen himself. Handsome, dignified, commanding, she had served Jansen as secretary and had superintended the work of the women. At the leader's death she knew the affairs of the colony better than any other and she promptly took over authority. But St. Paul had said, "Let your women keep silence in the churches," and among the Jansenites women were not allowed to speak in public. For that reason Andreas Borglund became her spokesman. But the difficulties of governing in silence were too great for her and soon the colony was incorporated under a committee of seven trustees.

Under the new direction the settlement prospered more than ever. New buildings, new industries were set up, the townsite was enlarged, and beautified by the planting of elm and black walnut saplings along the center ravine. New colonists came to greater fields. In 1855 the farmers plowed a cornfield in which the furrows were two miles long. A thousand acres of broomcorn were harvested; shipped to Peoria on consignment to Boston, the crop brought $50,000.

Meanwhile the twelve apostles were wandering over America teaching the Jansen gospel wherever folk would listen. One of the misionaries visited the Shakers at Pleasant Hill, Kentucky, and there his gospel met its better. Seeking converts, the apostle himself was converted. He promptly returned to Bishop Hill preaching the Shaker doctrine of celibacy. Back among his own people with this strange dogma, he met with such success that it was grafted onto the Jansen creed.

The end was near for the commune at Bishop Hill. The doctrine of celibacy aroused sharp conflict. It virtually put an end to family life, and it spelled ultimate extinction for the colony unless it could perpetuate itself by winning outside converts. Repelled by the new doctrine, many of the people moved away. Those who remained were torn by such dissension that all community worship was destroyed. The financial crisis of 1857 hastened the end. At last, in 1861, property to the amount of half a million dollars was divided among four hundred and fifteen shareholders, and Eric Jansen's folk scattered. Moving north and west over the Mississippi valley, they began to found communities for the great tide of Swedish settlement in America.

But the name of Eric Jansen's ardent adventure has not perished from memory. Bishop Hill, now a village of a few hundred souls, still marks the map of Illinois.

CHAPTER II

Towns in Stone and Towns on Paper

ALONG the Iowa shores of the Mississippi, at the towns of Guttenberg, McGregor, Bellevue and Lansing, are old houses built of native limestone by German settlers ninety years ago. From the beginning they must have had a look of permanence; now they appear fixed and ancient, as though rooted under the frowning bluffs. Other strains of people came, restless, to the Mississippi, quickly built their plain frame dwellings and after twenty years moved on to another border. But the Germans came to stay. It was a long way from the Rhine or the Elbe to the Mississippi shore, and when they had arrived their journeying was done. So in a timbered country, where lumber was used even for churches and river jetties, they patiently hewed out blocks of stone and slowly built their houses. Time and weather soon put a mark on the unpainted frame houses of the frontier; the board sidewalks were pitted with hobnail boots and the plank streets warped in the sun. But the German settlements stood solid, and today at Guttenberg (named for Johannes Gutenberg, the inventor of movable type, but misspelled in the first recorded plat of the townsite and so Guttenberg ever since) the old stone warehouses rise like a fortress beside the river where no more steamboats call, and the rows of stone houses, deep-doored and deep-casemented, are unchanged by time.

These towns, permanent like an Old World village, were not conceived so much as built, or they were conceived as the blocks took shape and the thick walls grew and the street was framed in solid, time-defying stone. There were other Mississippi River towns conceived in expectation. In the feverish years of the mid-century every cluster of huts had a prospect of future wealth and power, and in many an isolated shanty a man dreamed that the future would pave avenues across his pasture and plant a city on his fields.

There was a great energy in those years. People pushed into new regions, suffering hardship and surmounting immense difficulties. Settlements took shape in lonely places; while the wolves lurked in the forest and the Indians peered from the horizon, the citizens of future commonwealths thought of what the future would bring. Meanwhile they built their tentative roads or plowed a furrow to guide newcomers to them. From Mississippi River ports teamsters hauled freight into the interior of what was to become Iowa and Minnesota. From Dubuque the longest furrow in the world was plowed west to Iowa City; for a hundred miles Lyman Dillon guided a huge breaking plow behind five yoke of oxen. His furrow ran uphill and downhill, through thickets and across swales and over miles of virgin prairie that had never known a wheel mark or the gash of a plowshare. When it was done he had a mark to guide the roadbuilders, and a trail to lead settlers into new country before a road was there.

Into Iowa in 1855 came the Dubuque and Pacific Railroad. The corporation owned seven thousand building lots in the principal towns along the right-of-way across the newly formed state. But Dubuque was the only settlement of more than fifteen hundred population on the entire route beyond the Mississippi. In those years towns unknown in St. Louis were listed in the newspapers and building lots in port cities that no riverman had ever seen were advertised in the press of Dubuque and Galena. To some the future brought realization, and so Winona, La Crosse, Davenport, Burlington, Hastings became ports of entry and centers of culture and trade.

A few Mississippi River towns were conceived in deception and had their existence only on paper. Like the wildcat money that circulated up and down the river, there were titles to land in "paper cities" that changed hands among the speculators and brought poverty and disappointment to hopeful immigrants. The steamboat clerks in the 1850's were provided with a *Thompson's Bank Note Detector,* and along with it were lists of paper currency. One list included bills that were acceptable for business transactions, another listed bank notes not acceptable in any circumstance, a third list was made up of currency on which a clerk might speculate at rates from twenty-five to seventy-five per cent of the face value. There was never any attempt to list fraudulent real estate titles, but an experienced riverman knew that title to land in certain "townsites" was not worth the cost of printing. Scores of land sharks operated along the river, and they were frequently equipped with issues of "local" papers describing the business and social activity of the towns whose choice property they were prepared to sell. When the scheme was well-plotted and the materials well-planned, whole sections of riverfront prairie, unmarked by a single building or improvement, were sold at the rate of thousands of dollars an acre, before the proprietor had finished the pre-emption payments on the land he was reselling.

Such a paper town was Rollingstone City. It was located north of Winona, Minnesota, on one of the most beautiful sites of the Upper Mississippi; but the town existed only in the minds of speculators who sold town lots and farms in the community to hundreds of people in New York. In the spring of 1852 the Rollingstone colonists arrived at the port of Galena to take steamboat passage to their future home. When they could find no steamboat for Rollingstone City, they produced illustrated maps of an ordered and elaborate settlement with landing wharves, substantial business blocks, a hotel, a lecture hall, a library, and long rows of residential streets. Finally rivermen recalled a site three miles above Wabasha Prairie which seemed to correspond to the location of the plotted city. That region, only recently vacated by the Sioux, was empty except for a shanty belonging to a squatter named Johnson. There the Rollingstone settlers were landed and there they struggled to establish themselves. Being ignorant of farming and inexperienced in pioneer craft, they had a season of illness and discouragement before the community was abanboned. Rollingstone City never took shape on the Mississippi shore.

The most ambitious of chimerical townsites was the famous "future metropolis of the Mississippi," Nininger City, which was the dream and the fiasco of one of the memorable men on the upper river. In the spring of 1856 Ignatius Donnelly was twenty-five years old, and the river was vibrant with the hopes and enterprise of its most dramatic years. Railheads had reached the river and fleets of gleaming steamboats hurried with crowded decks and cabins to the landings of Wisconsin, Iowa, and Minnesota. Ignatius Donnelly, all his life a man intoxicated with the future, saw an empire of rich prairie, another empire of rich forest, and the sites of cities yet unborn. Most of all he saw the river. He watched stevedores singing on the levees, lurching across the landing stage with bacon, lard, whisky, plows, wagons, doors, window frames. He saw great log rafts of Upper Mississippi pine, the golden mounds of grain in the river barges, the ricks of lead on the sagging landings at Galena. Just one road was broad enough and firm enough to carry that commerce. So he recognized the Mississippi as the great highway of the West. He talked with hunters who described the riches of the country, elk, bear, venison, buffalo, grouse, quail, woodcock, prairie chicken. He heard of a hunter who had brought down forty-two ducks with a single charge of his shotgun and of farmers who killed pigeons with clubs and poles and then hitched their teams to heaping wagonloads of game. It was that kind of country; it was the future's country.

And so it was Ignatius Donnelly's. He had the buoyant nature, the expansive mind, the impulsive and idealistic spirit that made him, the moment he felt the mood of the Mississippi, a western man, and that even after his failure and disappointment kept him dreaming of the future. He was the laughingstock of saner and less sanguine men, but he was in tune with the great country and the great years. When the Gilded Age was past and the light of expectation faded, there was a headlong, headstrong, fact-defying illusion to remember. In more sober years America would recall it fondly, with amusement and some wistfulness, like a man smiling at the arduous folly of his youth. Mark Twain gave us Beriah Sellers to remember, and history gave us Ignatius Donnelly.

He was convinced that somewhere near the head of navigation on the Mississippi would rise the future metropolis of the Middle West. Deliberately he chose the site, a fine front of river for the future commerce, a level plateau for a business area, and a pleasing contour of upward-sloping land, commanding a noble view, for the residential districts. The location lay on the west bank of the Mississippi, twenty-five miles below St. Paul and five miles upstream from the busy town of Hastings. "Western towns have heretofore grown by chance," Donnelly said. But this city took shape in his imagination, ordered, spacious, dominant, with roads and river radiating from it in all directions. Here on a vacant hillside he envisoned one of the world's great cities.

With the capital and the collaboration of two Philadelphia men, John Nininger and Alexander Ramsey, he purchased the land, laid out the site, and was ready to sell building lots in the autumn of 1856. Donnelly plunged into a campaign of advertising, correspondence, public speaking—and his single, inexhaustible theme was "Nininger City." He struck off thousands of placards picturing a fast steamboat and a hurrying railway train (Nininger City was destined never to have a steamboat landing or to hear a locomotive whistle) and labeled EMIGRATION UP THE MISSISSIPPI RIVER. That winter

travelers in railway stations and hotels, in barbershops
and taverns, in steamboat offices and warehouses read
the glowing prospectus:

The attention of Emigrants and the Public generally, is called to the now rapidly improving TER-
RITORY OF MINNESOTA, containing a population of 150,000, and goes into the Union as a State
during the present year. According to an act of Congress passed last February, the State is munificently
endowed with Lands for Public Schools and State
Universities, also granting five per cent. on all sales
of U. S. Lands for Internal Improvements. On the
3d March, 1857, grants of Land from Congress was
made to the leading Trunk Railroads in Minnesota,
so that in a short time the trip from New Orleans
to any part of the State will be made in from two
and a half to three days. The CITY OF NIN-
INGER, situated on the Mississippi River, 35 miles
below St. Paul, is now a prominent point for a large
Commercial Town, being backed by an extensive
Agricultural, Grazing and Farming Country; has
fine streams in the interior, well adapted for Milling
in all its branches; and Manufacturing Water Power
to any extent. Mr. JOHN NININGER (a Gentleman of large means, ideas, and liberality, speaking
the various languages) is the principal Proprietor
of NININGER. He laid it out on such principles
as to encourage all MECHANICS, Merchants, or
Professions of all kinds, on the same equality and
footing; the consequence is, the place has gone ahead
with such rapidity that it is now an established
City, and will annually double in population for
years to come. Persons arriving by Ship or otherwise,
can be transferred without expense to Steamers go-

ing to St. Louis; or stop at Cairo and take Railroad
to Dunleith (on the Mississippi). Steamboats leave
Saint Louis and Dunleith daily for NININGER,
and make the trip from Dunleith in 36 to 48 hours.

As soon as he had distributed these placards Donnelly began circulating a "handsomely printed" plan of
the City of Nininger, Dacotah County, Minnesota,
which showed the city laid out in thirty streets, running
parallel with the river, and fifteen avenues named for
Donnelly and his friends.

On the first of December, 1856, appeared the
inaugural number of the *Emigrant Aid Journal*, Ignatius Donnelly, editor. The paper was printed in two
versions, English and German, at Philadelphia, but beneath a panoramic engraving picturing railroad trains,
steamboats and wagon caravans, wild cataracts, mounds
of fruit and sheaves of wheat, its heading carried
Nininger City, Minnesota Territory, along with
the date line. The paper emphasized the attractive features of Nininger City, of Minnesota, and of the Pre-
emption Act. A running head across the front page expressed Donnelly's love of classical learning as well as
his self-confidence. *"Dost thou know how to play the
fiddle?" "No," answered Themistocles, "but I understand the art of raising a little village into a great city."*

In January, 1857, before any settlers had arrived on
the vacant riverside, Donnelly published a "supplement"
to his plan of the city, enlarging it by a sizable addition
and therefore offering a widened choice of building lots.
Four other additions were plotted during the year.
Meanwhile thousands of descriptive folders were distrib-

uted through the mail to people in the East and in the
Ohio valley, and an arrangement was made with a line
of Atlantic steamers to recruit Scotch and English emigrants for Nininger City. Early in 1857, with the plans
all made, with property selling feverishly through the
mails, with the empty hillside waiting for its citizens,
Donnelly felt a little regretful that the labors of creating a metropolis were over. "Here I am," he wrote, "but
twenty-six years old, and I have already acquired a large
fortune. What shall I do to occupy myself the rest of
my life?"

That summer the steamboats carried puzzled passengers past the site of Nininger City because the landing which Donnelly had described had not yet taken
shape on the brushy river shores. The emigrants were put
ashore at Hastings and they made their way across three
miles of prairie to the future metropolis, which they had
trouble in locating. Though Donnelly had procured a
post-office designation for Nininger City, the mail for
his city was delivered at Hastings and the Nininger post-
master, Louis Loichot, tramped across country once a
week with a mail sack on his shoulder. When municipal
officers were chosen in Nininger, Ignatius Donnelly was
elected president of the town council. Under his leadership the civic body proceeded to provide an estray pen
for stray hogs, to let a contract for a public well, and to
order trees cut down so as to open the town to the view
of passing steamboats on the river.

Donnelly arranged a fitting celebration for the first
Fourth of July in Nininger City. The steamer *William
S. Nelson* was chartered to bring an excursion party
from St. Paul. When the boat arrived, four hours late,

the residents of Nininger cheered from the shore. A cannon in the bow of the steamer blasted a salute to the infant city, and blew off the mate's hand. After the guests were ashore a series of orations were delivered and a banquet was spread under the trees on the riverbank. The meal was followed by a program of seventeen speeches addressed to "The Future of Nininger," "The Pioneers of Minnesota," "The Great Yankee Nation," and other kindred topics. Before the program ended there was a fist fight between certain Nininger residents and some visitors from up the river.

By the autumn of 1857 Nininger claimed a population of five hundred. The "Mammoth Hotel" was being projected, along with a steam gristmill and a steam ferry to link Nininger with the east side of the Mississippi. Donnelly promised that the first railroad in Minnesota would soon come to Nininger, and he advocated the establishing of a public library, a public school, two churches, a social center, a seminary, and a lecture hall. Meanwhile the most impressive building in the town was Donnelly's own residence, a two-story, nine-room house surmounted by an "observatory" from which Nininger's founder could observe the growth of the metropolis.

But the glorious promise of Nininger ended that first year with the panic of 1857. The next spring weeds grew up in the plowed furrows that marked the city's streets, and one by one the discouraged families packed their goods and moved away. Several frame buildings were dismantled, moved to Hastings, and set up in the town that Nininger had been so confident of eclipsing. After a few more seasons there was nothing left of

Nininger City but Ignatius Donnelly's mansion. And Donnelly remained, yielding his belief in the future metropolis but retaining his love for the site above the curving Mississippi. He turned his building lots into wheatfields and called himself a farmer.

Donnelly was still a very young man; he had driving energy and a mind crowding with ideas. Two years later, at the age of twenty-eight, he was lieutenant governor of Minnesota, and for eight years in the sixties he served as a member of Congress. When his political career was ended he returned to his Nininger home and lived the life of a gentleman farmer and man of letters. He became celebrated as the author of strikingly bold and original books, and many people found their way to his spacious farmhouse to pay their respects to the "Sage of Nininger."

In the seventies and eighties one stretch of Upper Mississippi shore had two celebrated mansions, for Donnelly had a distinguished neighbor, a few miles downriver, in the person of General Israel Garrard, a Kentuckian who after the Civil War came to the bluffs of Minnesota and built a handsome southern home. He named it St. Hubert's Lodge, after the patron saint of hunters, and from its wide veranda he overlooked spacious lands which he ruled like a baron. To enjoy his hospitality and the lavish air of the Minnesota country there came to St. Hubert's Lodge a long list of visitors, including Henry Ward Beecher, Joseph Jefferson, and John La Farge. General Garrard, living aloof and splendid above the river, became a subject of legend, but Ignatius Donnelly remained the most celebrated figure on the Upper Missisippi until his death in 1901.

In his quiet years beside the river Donnelly was busy with ventures and speculations on paper, but this time it was in manuscript rather than in the platting of town lots. His books, espousing striking and unusual theories, sold hundreds of thousands of copies and brought an endless stream of visitors to his door. *Atlantis* argued the truth of Plato's fable of an Atlantic island where modern civilization originated. *Ragnarok: The Age of Fire and Gravel* was a sensationally popular pseudo-scientific explanation of the earth's ancient contact with a mighty comet. *The Great Cryptogram* proved by means of an elaborate cipher that Bacon wrote Shakespeare. So, with his far-ranging mind, dissatisfied with the accepted and familiar, speculating on the past and the future, the "Sage of Nininger" kept alive the name of the city that never came to be.

CHAPTER 12

The Saints at Nauvoo

COMMERCE CITY, Illinois, had a brief life, principally on paper. It was better known by a few eastern speculators who circulated engraved plats of the town than by rivermen who regularly steamed past the still unsettled shores of Hancock County. Just two board shanties comprised the "City" in 1839 when the Mormons arrived. They saw the rich Illinois fields waiting for industrious settlers, the terraced shore fit for a spacious town, and the solemn Mississippi, nearly two miles wide at that impressive point, ready to carry their commerce and to deliver converts to their landing. Quickly the Mormon agents bought fifty thousand acres and took possession.

This was a backtracking for the Saints. Already they had journeyed from Kirtland, Ohio, to Independence, Missouri, and from Independence, when the gentiles drove them out, to the town of Far West in a thinly settled region of the state. They settled there, but not for long. Again mobs attacked the faithful, and the faithful retaliated. When the Misosuri militia was called out they packed their goods for a new removal. Commerce City, Illinois, by a revelation to their founder, was the site ordained for them. So the harried Saints streamed back to the Mississippi. Across the broad river on the rising Illinois prairie they pitched their tents and planned the erection of their newest Zion.

Early in 1840 the name Commerce City was changed to Nauvoo, as more fitting to a community of Latter-Day Saints who were fulfilling Old Testament prophecies. Nauvoo was explained to the believers as a word of Hebrew origin meaning "Beautiful Place"—though a later scholar commented wryly on the Mormon name: "The nearest approach to Nauvoo in Hebrew is an adjective which would be translated *Naveh,* meaning 'pleasant,' a rather rare word. The letter correctly represented by *v* could not possibly do the double duty of *uv,* nor could *a* of the Hebrew ever be *au* in English, nor *eh* of the Hebrew be *oo* in English." He added, by way of suggesting a parallel derivation, that students of theology at Middletown, Connecticut, used to have a saying that that name was derived from Moses by dropping "oses" and adding "iddletown."

However hopefully it was named Nauvoo proved, during the first winter of its existence, to be a chill and fever-ridden place. As a result of strenuous efforts of Mormon missionaries, immigrants streamed in, some of them from the Midlands of England, four thousand miles away. They were unused to the severe Illinois seasons and unfit for the rigors of pioneer life. Many newcomers died during the first year of Nauvoo's eventful life. Afterward, Brigham Young remembered, from faraway Utah, the miraculous healing accomplished by Joseph Smith in that bleak first winter beside the Mississippi. "Joseph commenced in his own house and dooryard, commanding the sick, in the name of Jesus Christ, to arise and be made whole, and they were healed according to his word. He then continued to travel from house to house, healing the sick as he went."

When the winter was past and the Mississippi moved under the skies of May, Nauvoo grew at an astonishing rate. Nearly ten thousand people arrived during the year 1841, taking up their allotments in the spaciously planned town and finding their place in its busy life. Meanwhile the Mormons pushed their missionary campaigns, sending men "without purse or scrip" as the order required, to the eastern states and to foreign countries. Brigham Young was one of a vigorous corps of evangelists who journeyed from the Mississippi to the soot-stained cities of the English Midlands. There they labored with great success, winning converts, establishing a press to turn out their "Doctrine and Covenants" and beginning the publication of the *Millennial Star*. Other missionaries were at work in Amsterdam, Constantinople, and Jerusalem, in Australia and the islands of the Pacific. The chief appeal of the Mormon evangelists was to the poor. Such people, ignorant, superstitious, economically insecure, were quick to accept the initiation into the "secrets" of revelation and were eager to migrate to any place, however distant, where a plot of land was promised to them. Migration from England was stimulated by the prediction that soon the sea would be dried up between Liverpool and New York, after which the journey to America would be impossible, and by descriptions of the throngs of pilgrims in mile-long wagon trains already on their way to the new Zion beside the Mississippi. The Mormon settlement was described in glowing terms, one detail being that the Lord had rained down manna on a ten-acre field outside Nauvoo; it was like wafers dipped in honey and it fell so profusely that people could not gather it all.

The result of these efforts was that thousands of English converts took pasage, in ships chartered by Mormon agents, across the Atlantic. At New York other agents met them and led them to the West. Some vessels sailed direct to New Orleans, where the immigrants transferred to river steamers and ascended the Mississippi to Nauvoo. So the town grew over the grasslands of Hancock County.

With Nauvoo firmly established, Joseph Smith released the longest of the "revelations" by which he made God's will known to his followers. As in previous revelations, this one announced that Joseph Smith was to be "a presiding elder over all my church, to be a translater, a revelator, a seer and a prophet." It included, further, detailed instructions for the erecting of a temple (the Mormons had already left three temples to mark their wanderings) of magnificent size and style. Work on the building began immediately, along with other movements such as the forming of a military force called the Nauvoo Legion, which by its size, equipment, and discipline alarmed occasional visiting army officers who could compare it with the state militias of the West. When the cornerstone of the temple was laid Joseph Smith put aside his roles of seer and prophet and appeared as lieutenant general, with four aides-de-camp and twelve stalwart guards, at the head of his smartly marching Legion.

The temple, designed to be "the most magnificent religious edifice in the world," was built by the patient

labor and sacrifice of people who lived in rude cabins
and cheerfully delivered their tithes, even to implements
and articles of clothing, to the officials of the church.
There were, however, members of the community who
had lucrative sources of revenue. The presence of coun-
terfeiters was repeatedly rumored among the Mormons,
and there were frontier thieves and desperadoes who had
joined the religious colony for protection, bringing
stolen goods with them. It was reported that they held it
was right to steal from anyone not belonging to the
church, provided one-third of the stolen property was
consecrated to the building of the temple.

When completed in 1846 the temple was an impos-
ing and barbarous structure of mingled Romanesque,
Greek, and Egyptian architecture. It was built of native
white limestone at a cost which the Mormons estimated
at a million dollars. Around the portico rose thirty
polished stone pilasters, the capital of which represented
the sun emerging from a cloud along with two hands
holding a trumpet. At the base of the great tower large
golden letters announced "The House of the Lord, built
by the Church of Latter Day Saints. Commenced April
6, 1841. Holiness to the Lord." At the pinnacle of the
spire stood a gilded figure of the angel Moroni, who had
revealed to Joseph Smith the burial place of the golden
plates on the Palmyra hillside in New York State and to
whom, therefore, all the Mormon revelations were due.
The completed temple, with its various rooms and halls
and its notable baptismal basin, four feet deep and supported by twelve carved oxen of life size, corresponded
to the architectural "revelation" which had come to
Joseph Smith that first winter in Nauvoo.

With his community flourishing and the state of Illinois already acknowledging the power of the Mormons, Joseph Smith began to express views on national politics. Declaring that liberty was on the wane in the United States, he proposed specific remedies for that condition. Among other reforms he suggested reducing the membership of Congress by half, cutting the pay of congressmen to two dollars a day and board, pardoning all convicts in state and federal prisons, and purchasing the freedom of the slaves with funds from the sale of public lands.

One week after his initial expression of political views the Nauvoo *Times and Seasons* announced that Smith was the Mormon candidate for the presidency of the United States. From that day until his death by violence four months later, the *Times and Seasons* carried at its masthead in bold block letters:

For President
GENERAL JOSEPH SMITH
Nauvoo, Illinois

Smith sent a body of two thousand Mormon missionaries through the eastern and southern states to conduct a political campaign. Besides being shrewd, ambitious, and aggressive, he had other qualifications for political success. Though he enjoyed his role as "translater and revelator" he had the common touch and he moved with ease among his followers. In his journals, along with entries that concern his religious revelations, there appear such notes as "Played ball with the brethren," and he sometimes offered to engage in wrestling matches with his official colleagues. He was a man of impressive stature, six feet tall, weighing more than two hundred pounds. No one accepted his challenges.

At Nauvoo in the year 1843 Smith made known to a few officers of the church a fresh revelation which sanctioned plural marriages. At first this was not proclaimed publicly, but the doctrine of celestial marriage began to find its way among the believers. A number of the Mormon leaders were "sealed" to new and various wives by the authority of the church. But vigorous opposition to this doctrine was expressed by a few subordinates, and Smith found himself for the first time facing a stormy resistance within his own order. A newspaper, the Nauvoo *Expositor*, was established in direct opposition to Smith and his character and doctrines were attacked in its columns. By his orders the offending press was destroyed, and the leaders of the opposition fled across the Illinois prairie to Carthage.

As the story of their flight and the destruction of their property became known, a wave of anti-Mormon feeling spread throughout the state. When the fugitives entered complaint for the violence done them, warrants were issued for the arrest of Joseph Smith and his brother Hyrum. In due time the writ was presented at Nauvoo, where it was quickly set aside by the Mormon authorities.

Such defiance of law and order aroused the spirit of the frontier communities. At Warsaw, Illinois, eighteen miles down the Mississippi, it was formally resolved that if the prophet and his miscreant colleagues were not surrendered, "a war of extermination should be waged, to the entire destruction, if necessary for our protection, of his adherents." In neighboring towns military companies were quickly organized and Governor Ford of Illinois made a hurried visit to Carthage in an attempt to arrange a legal and orderly trial of the Mormon leaders.

Back at Nauvoo, Joseph Smith was having some hard thoughts. Though he was still in authority there, he was aware that doubt and dissension among the Saints had imperiled his hold upon them. Many of his stanchest and ablest colleagues, men upon whom he could have depended in this crisis, were far away from Nauvoo, having been sent out to lay a foundation for his presidential campaign. As it was, he doubted the successful outcome of a contest with the state of Illinois. So, on the night of June 22nd, he started with his brother Hyrum and a few followers for the distant wilderness sanctuary of the Rocky Mountains. He had no more than crossed the Mississippi, however, before he was intercepted by friends who persuaded him that he must not desert his people. Thereupon he returned to Nauvoo and submitted to arrest.

By this time there were other charges besides the original complaint over the destruction of the rival Nauvoo newspaper; Smith was now charged with treason, by his act of declaring martial law in Nauvoo and calling out his Legion to combat the authority of the state. Under that charge he and his confederates were taken to Carthage and secured in the county jail. Meanwhile Carthage was seething with militiamen who were determined to march on Nauvoo, ostensibly to search for a counterfeiting establishment, but with the real purpose of razing the city and driving the Mormons across the river. Governor Ford was equally determined to prevent such a move, not only because it would mean a reign of violence but because he could not be sure that the militia was a match for the powerful Nauvoo Legion. He finally succeeded in disbanding all but three companies, two of which were left to guard the Carthage jail while the third accompanied the governor on an orderly visit to the Mormon city.

While the governor was on this errand, a dramatic episode unfolded in the gray stone jailhouse at the edge of the straggling town of Carthage. In a large room on the second floor of the jail Joseph Smith and his colleagues were lounging on a row of cots. Through an open door they saw a file of men with blackened faces coming up the stairway. Instantly the Mormons closed the door and braced their shoulders against it. Rifle bullets crashed through the panel and Hyrum Smith fell to the floor. "I am a dead man," he said. He did not move again.

Joseph Smith now produced a concealed pistol and fired through the hallway. Though the door was allowed to swing ajar, the attackers hesitated to come in. But they fired into the room, injuring two of the Mormons. Smith made a dash for the window, twenty-five feet above the ground. Before he could clamber through the opening three rifle balls struck him. He fell outward, crying, "O Lord, my God!"

One story (there are several) has it that Smith was not dead when he fell into the jailyard. Wounded and dazed he gathered himself after his fall, leaning against a stone well curb. Then a squad of men leveled their rifles at him. When the smoke cleared away Joe Smith was dead. The stories all agree on that.

With Smith's death the lynchers were satisfied. They left two other Mormons cringing in the jail and carried the bodies of the Smith brothers to the Carthage Hotel at the center of the town. The next day the bodies were taken to Nauvoo. The Mormons received them quietly, with bewilderment and grief. Graves were dug and coffins lowered into the ground. But when a grave robbery occurred the next night all that the robbers found were two boxes filled with stones. Secretly the Mormons buried the Prophet and his brother beneath the temple; shortly afterward, fearing the discovery of so obvious a burial place, they reburied them under the brick wall of the Nauvoo House on the bank of the Mississippi.

Smith's assailants were indicted, in due time, yet there were never any prosecutions. The guards at the jail refused to identify them and witnesses gave hopelessly conflicting accounts of what had happened on that feverish June day. But according to Mormon legend, the death of the Prophet was mysteriously avenged: The commandant of the guards at the Carthage jail was fatally shot within a year. The governor's prosecutor, who failed to bring the lynchers to justice, was assasssinated twenty-four years later. One of the assailants, who had been struck by a bullet from the Prophet's pistol, carried a wounded arm that continued to rot long afterward; finally it was amputated, and even then it would not heal. Another of his assailants died horribly, a few years later, after crossing the plains to California; he was "eaten by worms." Still another suffered for years from a loathsome facial disease until at last "half his face fell off."

With Joseph Smith's death a dramatic chapter in the Mormons' story was ended, and another equally dramatic was about to begin. But not beside the Mississippi. In January, 1845, the state of Illinois repealed the Nauvoo charter, and during the following season hostility toward the Mormons gathered again. Under the vital leadership of Brigham Young the Saints prepared to journey to the distant West. All property which they could not carry with them they sold or abandoned where it stood; the rest they made ready for the journey. That winter there was a great restlessness beside the river. The air was filled with the sound of saws and the clatter of hammers; wagonmakers, wheelwrights, blacksmiths, carpenters toiled day and night. In February, 1846, Brigham Young led the first caravan, fifteen hundred men, women, and children, across the ice-fast Mississippi. During the spring the Mormons left at the rate of a thousand every week. In early summer, after dedicating the newly completed temple, the last caravan crossed the river and began the long and weary march to Utah. Behind them they left a deserted city.

For three years it was a ghost town, the largest city on the Mississippi lying silent and lifeless in the encircling bend of the river. Weeds grew up in the streets and rabbits nibbled at the rank gardens. On a November night in 1848 a band of incendiaries, still wrathful though the Mormon town was an empty shell, stole through the lifeless streets and set fire to the temple. It was left a gutted ruin.

But Nauvoo was to become the scene of another

fervent society. In 1849 the Icarians came up the Mississippi from their failure in Texas. Under the founder of
the society, the French reformer Etienne Cabet himself,
they set up their communistic order in the vacant Mormon town. Buildings were there for them to occupy,
fields were ready for their tillage. Cabet began to re-
build the temple, but a spring cyclone in 1850 demol-
ished it. Though the Icarians made a prosperous beginning there, dissension followed. In 1856 Cabet himself
was expelled. The colony disbanded a few years later.

Then Nauvoo settled down to the life of a secular
Illinois village. After the Civil War families filtered in,
simple families bent not on founding Zion or Utopia
but only on making a home amid the fertile fields beside the river. Many of them were German immigrants,
practical, thrifty, industrious. They used the stone
blocks of the temple as the foundation of stables and
houses. They plowed the earth and planted it. Now their
descendants live in a quiet village encircled by fruitful
fields and orchards. On the crest of the hill there is
nothing to mark the site of the "most magnificent religious edifice in the world." Two of the Mormon buildings are left, as museums, containing relics of a hundred
years ago. And there are other relics—a few ruined
houses with weathered walls and boarded windows and
a tangle of trumpet vine reaching up to the sagging
rooftree.

CHAPTER 13

The Steamboat Age

Through the warm weeks of midsummer, 1817, the people of the sprawling town of St. Louis often looked down the empty river curving between the lush green shores. They knew that among the fleets of keelboats and flatboats passing down the Ohio and the Lower Mississippi there now moved the noisy new steamboats, with their paddlewheels churning the water and their tall stacks smoking against the sky. In the spring of 1817 eight new steamers had been launched on the Ohio, and word found its way to St. Louis that a steamboat was scheduled to breast the Mississippi current to its landing. The merchants speculated on the day of her arrival and what cargo she would bring. Men on the water front argued whether she would appear at all. The height of expectation passed, and no paddle wheels had troubled the river along the St. Louis levee. There was a cheated feeling in the city; the river was vacant as the summer sky and the steamboat was a broken promise.

Then on a windless August day a blue haze of woodsmoke hung in the sky below the bend of the river. It darkened. It drew near. Around the bend came the *Zebulon M. Pike*, her paddle wheels splashing, with a scroll of water at her bow.

She was a small boat, clumsy as a barge, with no

paddle casings and no deckhouse. It took her six weeks to make the journey from Louisville to St. Louis. Her low-pressure engine propelled her at three miles an hour, except in a hard current. For that emergency the crew took their stations on the running boards and poled her as they would a scow. But she was a steamboat and she had found St. Louis. When she docked at the foot of Market Street most of the city's five thousand citizens were on the levee to welcome her.

Another historic day for St. Louis and the Upper Mississippi was April 21, 1823. On that spring day the stern-wheeler *Virginia*, with steam up and smoke blowing from her stacks, lay at the levee loading the last barrel of goods for the lonely stations on the upper river. Except at St. Louis, the Upper Mississippi was still beyond the fringe of settlement. The prosperous river cities were yet unfounded, or they consisted of a squatter's hut or a half-breed trader's shanty on the shore. But the northern army posts depended on supplies from downriver, and the *Virginia* was the first steamboat to set out with supplies for the scattered posts.

Under Captain John Crawford the *Virginia* churned into the stream, as a crowd of Indians and immigrants, teamsters and fur traders watched from the levee. In her boxlike deck cabin the *Virginia* housed a few passengers, a short list but a memorable one. Giacomo Constantine Beltrami, the romantic Italian adventurer, had secured passage to Fort Snelling, where he planned to launch his own expedition to discover the source of the Mississippi. A keen and never sated observer, he kept a journal which provides a chronicle of the *Virginia*'s famous voyage, a chronicle dignified with

Beltrami's classical learning and made vivid by his enthusiasm for the wilderness shores of the great valley and the glimpses of frontier and savage life along the way. Another passenger was Major Lawrence Taliaferro, Indian agent at Fort Snelling, now on the way back to his post after a few months' absence. Taliaferro was a man of Italian extraction and he found a ready bond with Beltrami; they had in common a restlessness, a romantic feeling for the great river, and a courtly manner that must have seemed strange in the rude western country. Sharing the narrow cabin with them was a bold Sauk chief, Great Eagle, who had overcome the fears of his tribesmen (they called the steamboat Great Medicine and fled at its approach) and was about to make a journey up the river whose banks he had so often trod. A family of Kentuckians, surrounded by cats, dogs, hens and turkeys, sat on deck. They were on their way to the lead mines at Galena—as was a final passenger, a lone woman missionary who planned to work among the Wisconsin Indians.

It was not a speedy passage. Once a day Captain Crawford chose a likely landing spot and the *Virginia* came to rest along the shore. The crew jumped off, brandishing axes, and proceeded to cut firewood for the steamboat's boilers. On one such stop Beltrami, anxious for the feel of exploration, wandered off in the forest and became lost. When he found his way back to the river the *Virginia* was gone; Captain Crawford had not checked the passenger list after the fuel was loaded. But the steamboat had struck a sand bar a little distance ahead, and when the explorer fired a distress signal with his gun, a canoe put off from the *Virginia* to take him aboard. Meanwhile Great Eagle was pacing the deck in disgust. He became so impatient with the pilot's ignorance and the boat's impeded progress that he waded ashore and continued his journey on foot in the traditional Sauk manner. He must have felt triumphant the next day, for when the white man's invention came puffing in to Fort Edwards, at the mouth of the Des Moines River, Great Eagle was on the landing waving to his former traveling companions.

Two dangerous passages lay ahead of the *Virginia*—the Lower, or Des Moines, Rapids and the Upper Rapids abreast of Rock Island. With a combination of boldness and good fortune, and the aid of a lightened cargo, Captain Crawford took his craft successfully through the first stretch, nine miles long, of rocks and swirling water. At Fort Armstrong, on Rock Island, the *Virginia* discharged more cargo. That fact, and the circumstance that the river had been rising for two days, made it possible to navigate the longer and swifter Upper Rapids; but the task was so laborious that when the danger was past Captain Crawford beached his boat to give his crew a rest.

After stops at Galena and Prairie du Chien the *Virginia* steamed on through the dramatic upper valley, impressing the Indians on the way, until at last she turned into the Minnesota River under the cliffs of Fort Snelling. She had come eight hundred miles in twenty days, lying up at night, stopping to cut all her firewood, fighting her way through the rapids, tediously removing herself from sand bars. She had done what many men said was impossible. With her rumbling boilers and clumsy paddle wheels she had ascended the Upper Mississippi.

Times changed rapidly in the western country a hundred years ago. In 1823 the voyage of the *Virginia* was a wonder; but the wonder soon became a commonplace. For by 1830 the steamboat age had come to the upper river, and by 1840 there was a never-ending pageant of commerce between St. Louis and the head of navigation at St. Anthony's Falls.

This steam traffic on the upper river was a triumph of men more than of machines. The boats improved in size and in engine power; in fact the trade evolved great vessels like the *Grey Eagle,* the *Key City,* and the *Northern Light.* With brass bands playing in the lounges and tall mirrors in the barrooms reflecting the cosmopolitan life of traders, army officers, speculators, travelers, these boats were floating palaces in their time. But the passage of the river channels, with the maze of islands, the shifting bars, and the long dangerous rapids, remained a matter of human judgment, skill, and courage.

The first steamboats that followed the *Virginia* up the uncharted river, long before there were any channel markers and before a river lore had developed around landmarks, bends and islands, were piloted by men who knew how to read the face of the water and understood the laws of flow of a great river. By the old reckoning, before the channel was straightened with wing dams and dikes, the distance from St. Louis to St. Paul was eight hundred miles, every one of which offered steamboatmen a test of their manhood. It took alertness and vigilance, it required lightning decisions and steady nerves to bring their vessels through. Any innocent stretch of water might mask submerged rocks or sunken bars, around any hidden bend might lurk snags and shoals. Under those conditions piloting was not so much a trade as a miracle. It is no wonder that, after they were gone from the river, men remembered the famous pilots like Louis de Marah, Louis Moreau, and Pleasant Carmack, who took the first steamboats up the Mississippi.

Even when boats were better built and the river's landmarks had meaning in terms of deep or shoal water, crosscurrents or a sluggish stream, there remained bad places, unpredictable stretches of river and other stretches all too predictable in their tricky currents and sharply turning channels. "Nightmares," the pilots called them, and they had a list long enough to fill a cub pilot's heart with dismay. The worst of them all were the well-cursed stretches at Cassville, Brownsville, Trempeleau, Rollingstone, Beef Slough, Point Douglass, Boulanger's Island, Grey Cloud, and Pig's Eye. To say any of those names was enough to give a steamboatman a bad dream.

Famous pilots in the 1850's, the great years of the river trade, were Thomas Cushing, Ned West, Thomas Burns, William Fisher, John King. They practiced their calling before improvements came to the river, but not before the Upper Mississippi had become one of the great transportation routes of America. When towns were mushrooming along the river, when freight was piled at every levee, and when passengers swarmed onto boats bound for the newly opened territories of Iowa and Minnesota, a steamboat was worth money in proportion to the number of trips she could make. These pilots all held records for getting a boat upriver in the shortest time. They were well-paid, eight hundred dollars a month, and they were worth it. They took boats of three hundred and four hundred tons through eight hundred miles of channel, despite changing banks, reefs, bars, snags, shoals, sunken wrecks, and a level of water never two trips or two days the same. They had no comforting range lights on a starless night, no "diamond boards" to steer by in the daytime. They didn't even have a searchlight, only a smelly smoking torch held on the end of a stick, almost worse than darkness. They had to know the shore outlines for all those hundreds of miles— bluffs, hills, knobs, islands, bars, beaches; they even had to know individual treetops silhouetted against the sky. They had to know the hidden channel and then how to handle their engines so as to keep the boat in safe water. At Coon Slough going downstream a side-wheeler made the sharp bend with one paddle wheel backing while the other churned ahead; a stern-wheeler backed against the point and let the current swing her bow. There were dozens of such places, each requiring its particular and exact maneuver.

On the upper river the boats used a sounding pole instead of the familiar lead line. On the bow the leadsman stood thrusting his notched pole for bottom. "No-o-o bottom! No-o-o bottom!" meant more than twelve feet of water. "Mar-r-k Twain!" indicated the depth of the sounding pole, twelve feet or two fathoms. Upper Mississippi pilots were not alarmed by the cry of "Eight and a half!" or even of six feet. They were used to shallow water. They had hundreds of miles of it.

Despite the greatest skill in her handling, a boat might hang up daily on some bar or shoal. Then it had to be "sparred off"—a simple term for a strenuous and risky undertaking. It involved the use of great poles of straight-grained Norway pine, the pent-up strength of a donkey engine, and a heartbreaking lunge of man-power—all timed so exactly as to lift the steamer off the bar without "hogging" her, which meant without breaking the hull or bending it out of shape. In the upper river were places where a boatman could not expect enough water to keep him off bottom. At best it was a case of sliding over, and even the smallest deviation from course meant running hard aground. At certain points it was common practice to haul the vessel over a bar by pulling on a line made fast to a tree on the bank or by securing an anchor in the river bed ahead and hauling the boat toward it. When these methods failed freight had to be transferred and the vessel lightened so that she would float free. But there were times when even that measure was not enough; occasionally a boat was stranded so high out of water that the only way to float her again was to build a crib under her for a second launching. This required weeks of labor, and a second launching, from some mosquito-clouded sand bar in a breathless stretch of river, was far from the festive ceremony of the first.

A captain could pilot his boat on the river when he chose to, but by an unwritten law a captain, even though he had a pilot's license, could not interfere with the pilot's authority. Often the captain had served his time as a pilot, and in many cases he owned a share of the vessel under his command. But in a tight place on

the river, when decisions must be made positively and
quickly, it was the pilot who made them. The captain
had other authority—over the demeanor and business
within the boat itself. His cabin in the forward part of
the "texas," beneath the pilothouse, served as office, con-
ference room, and observation room; from its banks of
windows he had a sweeping view of the river and of the
forward portion of his boat. His sleeping quarters were
directly under the pilothouse; in all hours of the day or
night he could hear and feel the vital life of the vessel,
footsteps moving overhead, the creaking of steering gear
as the big wheel moved under the pilot's hands, the bells
ringing, the leadsman's voice calling up from the boat's
blunt bow, the roar of flames in the twin tall chimneys.

Both pilots and captains were aristocrats on the
river. Wherever they went authority accompanied them.
Men afloat, whether crew or passengers, were subor-
dinate to them, and men ashore looked to them atten-
tively and listened with respect. They had the manner
of men who do big and important things, and they
moved up and down the dramatic valley in a steamboat's
splendor.

For the big steamers of the great years just before
the Civil War were splendid creations. They had gleaming white cabins scalloped in scrollwork and gleaming
black chimneys joined by a monkey brace that was
spangled with brass balls. They had an aloof and spacious
texas and a castellated pilothouse. In the long mahogany
saloons were series of panels depicting noted landscapes
of the river, such scenes as Lover's Leap, Maiden Rock,
Mount Trempeleau, Dayton Bluff, and the Falls of St.
Anthony.

The big side-wheelers carried their names painted with a sunburst on the great paddle boxes, or framed in heroic golden eagles, black eagles, spread eagles. The *Minnesota's* paddle box carried the new state's coat of arms in lavish colors. The *Minnesota Belle* pictured a western maid, many times life size, proudly carrying a bundle of grain and a reaping hook. The *Northern Belle* pictured another girl of the Golden West. The *General Brooke* and the *Phil Sheridan* showed heroic portraits of their namesakes; Little Phil was mounted on his charger, and for ten seasons he galloped up and down the Mississippi on the paddle boxes of a packet.

Besides the vessel's crew and a noisy gang of stevedores, the big boats carried musical organizations for their passengers' pleasure. A few of them boasted a full brass band; they moved in music, and the people of lonely river settlements trooped down to the water's edge to listen while the lordly boat steamed past. Many of them carried orchestras, with individual musicians whose reputations almost rivaled the pilot's, and had more commercial appeal. Ned Kendall was such a man; his cornet, famous on the river for a dozen years before he succumbed completely to drink, made any boat popular. Further entertainment was provided by Negro choruses, waiters, barbers, and porters doubling on stringed instruments and as vocalists. They gave concerts in the saloon and on moonlit nights they sang from the lower deck while the passengers lined the rail above. Under the northern hills they sang the plantation melodies of the South, and they seemed to make the great river one, so that the dark forests of Minnesota faded into the cottonfields and the languorous bayous of Louisiana.

But the river produced its own songs, too, and many a traveler remembered the rich laughter and the childish wonder that welled up in the Negro voices while the dark river slid past.

> De Captain stands on de upper deck
>   (Ah ha-a-a-ah! Oh ho-o-o-ho!)
> You nebber see nudder such gen'lehem, I spec;
>   (Ah ha-a-a-ah! Oh ho-o-o-ho!)
>
> De pilot he twisses de big roun wheel
>   (Ah ha-a-a-ah! Oh ho-o-o-ho!)
> He sings an he whissels an he dance Virginny reel;
>   (Ah ha-a-a-ah! Oh ho-o-o-ho!)
>
> Gineer in de engine room lissen for de bell
>   (Ah ha-a-a-ah! Oh ho-o-o-ho!)
> He boun to beat dat oder boat or bus em up to—
>   heben!
>   (Ah ha-a-a-ah! Oh ho-o-o-ho!)
>
> De debbel he come in de middle of de night
>   (Ah ha-a-a-ah! Oh ho-o-o-ho!)
> Sam, dere, he scairt so he tuhns mo's white!
>   (Ah ha-a-a-ah! Oh ho-o-o-ho!)

The logical extreme in musical entertainment came with the calliope. The *Excelsior* was the first boat on the upper river to have a "steam piano," and it was good business. But many a traveler, lured to the *Excelsior* by the gaudy tunes that sounded so fine amid the bustle of embarking, cursed the melodious outburst at three A.M.

Captain Ward of the *Excelsior* was pleased with his new plaything and he sounded a tune for every town on the river, no matter at what hour the boat was going by.

One of the most lucrative posts on the big boats was that of the bartender, who usually leased the bar as a private concession and handled his business independently. When the vessels were crammed with restless, convivial travelers the bar was busy around the clock and money flowed like water into the bartender's till. Billy Henderson of St. Louis started in as bartender of the *Excelsior* and later kept the bar on the lavish *Metropolitan*. He was so successful that when the Northern Line was organized he leased the bars on all the boats of the line and staffed them with his own men. In a few years he made a fortune.

A successful bartender had to be a shrewd and skillful man, a judge of human nature as well as of bottled spirits. He had to know, without being told, what drinks were appropriate and appealing to his varied clientele—mint juleps for southern gentlemen, whisky highballs for eastern merchants, bankers and speculators, straight whisky four fingers deep for Westerners. One of the shady tricks of the trade was to make "French brandy" by mixing burnt peach stones, cod-liver oil, and nitric acid with new Kentucky whisky. This cheap synthetic mix was a popular drink with rugged and unsophisticated palates, and a bartender could dispense gallons of it if he chose his patrons shrewdly.

But not all the variety of life on the riverboats was to be found in the noise and glitter of the barroom. In the forties and fifties a great tide carried people to the West, people of all kinds and persuasions. Speculators, schoolmasters, lumbermen, railroadmen, soldiers, miners, gamblers, missionaries—the river brought them to the bustling towns from which the first roads in Missouri, Iowa, and Minnesota led to the newly opened country. Every northbound boat was crowded; some carried as many as a thousand persons, with passengers spreading their bedding on the cabin floor and on the deck outside. As fast as they could make the run, the boats came down to load again. Swarms of people were always waiting for passage at St. Louis, at Rock Island, at Dunleith (now East Dubuque, Illinois), at Prairie du Chien, and at La Crosse. Roads reached these embarking points in the thirties, and railroads in the fifties. But there was neither road nor railroad paralleling the river, and the boats had the whole urgent commerce to carry.

The rush of immigration, which began after the Black Hawk War in 1832, reached a climax after the momentous year 1848, when the potato famine in Ireland and the abortive revolution in Germany sent hundreds of thousands of immigrants to the Mississippi valley. Throngs of people in the homespun garments of the Old World, wooden chests on their shoulders and portmaneaus in their hands, streamed through Chicago. Passenger trains with two locomotives brought long chains of immigrant cars, and the immigrant boats on the Great Lakes carried an even greater traffic from Buffalo to ports on the western shore of Lake Michigan. So the Lakes cities grew and the prairie counties filled up and thousands of new settlers pushed on to the Mississippi and beyond. In 1856 nine thousand immigrants changed trains at Chicago in a single day, and at the same time the Milwaukee and Mississippi and the Milwaukee and La Cross Railroads were carrying other thousands to the river ports. There throngs of Germans, Irish, Norwegians, Bohemians, Swedes waited restlessly for the steamboats that would carry them to the rich lands above. They filled the railway stations and the steamboat offices, covering the floor with a solid mat of chests, trunks and bundles, and lying down to sleep in the midst of their goods.

Immigrant passage up the river was made "on deck," which meant on the lower deck, exposed both to the heat of the boilers and to the vagaries of weather, as the lower deck stood wide open at the forward end. When scores of families were crowded into this space, sanitation was difficult and contagion was inevitable. Cholera was a not infrequent passenger on the lower deck; despite quarantine regulations and such remedies as burnt cork and a few drops of peppermint in a spoonful of brandy, along with the widely used "Indian Vegetable Pills," the disease broke out sporadically on the riverboats for twenty years. The crew might leap ashore at an unscheduled landing, far from any town, and hastily dig a victim's grave. Other times, under cover of darkness, bodies were dropped without ceremony into the stream. Rumors of epidemic on certain vessels brought them a reputation as "pest boats," a designation that might linger for years. But the urgent ranks of immigrants, new to America, looking at the Mississippi for the first time, did not know the lore of the steamboat lines and did not hesitate to crowd aboard the first boat that appeared.

However unsanitary, the lower deck presented a

picturesque sight in those expanding years. Along with the immigrants were all their possessions, and these included horses and cattle, pigs and chickens, wagons and plows, as well as beds and cradles and boxes of kitchenware. The new families sat amidst their goods staring at the moving shores of America, dreaming of the earth they would mark with their own corner stakes and plow with their own furrows.

A daily problem in the steamboat business was the acquiring of fuel. A big boat burned from thirty to forty cords of hardwood every twenty-four hours and its bunker space was limited to a day's supply. Consequently, every day was "wooding up" day, and that became a lively incident aboard the vessels as well as an important pioneer industry along the shore.

An acre of good woodland provided a hundred cords of wood, for which steamboatmen paid $2.50 a cord. Upland wood was run down the bluff in chutes and then was cut and piled on the riverbank. It was piled in four-foot lengths, eight feet high, in ranks of eighty-four feet with a cross-piled "cob-house" at each end—twenty cords of fuel to a rank. To see that the boat got sound wood and honest measure was the second clerk's responsibility. When a steamer pulled into a woodyard the mud-clerk (second clerk) jumped ashore and measured the ranks with an eight-foot stick. He had to judge quickly, with an eye for rotten or inferior wood, for short lengths or for sticks that were piled irregularly. Ten lengths of the measuring stick equaled twenty cords, if fairly piled. Honest and careful woodmen made their ranks eighty-four feet to allow for shortage and loose piling. Such a woodman was invited aboard to "have one on the mate" while the fuel was being loaded. But there were many "pirate" woodyards where a mud-clerk had to be on constant watch for short measure and green wood. Even Huck Finn was critical of that kind of business; he commented on a woodyard "piled by them cheats so you can throw a dog through it anywheres." The mud-clerk had to discount their ranks to nineteen, eighteen and a half, or eighteen cords, and then he had to argue with them. Often the pirate was an illegal dealer, cutting wood on government land and ready to move on ahead of federal agents.

The best fuel wood came from upland fields, where farmers were clearing cropland. The wood business brought them a cash income while they prepared their ground for plowing, and it provided the steamboats with fine sound fuel, solid logs of maple, ash, hickory, and split white oak. With that to feed fires an engineer could keep his boiler gauges quivering.

In the rush, flush seasons boats loaded wood on the run from barges in midstream. The barge was made fast to the steamboat's lower deck and was towed along for half an hour while the stevedores carried the wood aboard. Then the barge cast off and drifted back to the woodyard. In seasons of high water there was an inevitable shortage of fuel; when the woodyards were flooded a whole winter's crop of firewood drifted down the swollen current.

Until 1860 there was a marked division of labor between Negro and white crews on the Upper Mississippi boats. The cabin crews, consisting of waiters and porters, and the firemen were Negroes; the roustabouts and stevedores that made up the deck crew were invariably white. These deck crews were mostly Irish; the same breed of tough and laughing laborers that dug the dredge ditches and canals and laid the railroad ties of the new country, handled the endless flow of boxed, baled, and barreled freight on the Upper Mississippi. They lived hard and worked hard, they ate like wolves and slept like bears. In every kind of weather they tumbled out to "spar" the boat off a shoal, to heave the wood aboard, to lug the cargo up the landing stage. Normally they ate and slept in a crowded bunkroom on the lower deck, but on wet nights, after handling freight or wooding up, they crawled under the boilers till the clothes had dried on their bodies.

A big boat carried a deck crew of forty men, picked up from the levees of St. Louis, Galena, Dubuque, and St. Paul. As most cargoes included some barreled whisky, the crew had to be watched night and day. When they managed to broach a barrel by handling it too roughly, no power on earth could keep them from salvaging the escaping liquor. Then they became fighting drunk and mutinous. A mate had to be ready with a revolver in one hand and a stave in the other. After the Civil War the deck crews were made up of Negroes, and the Irish became mates. They made good mates, sharp-tongued, hard-fisted, ready for any task or trial.

The upper river did not permit the great racing tradition that became famous in Lower Mississippi lore. With its intricate channel and scant depth the river above St. Louis, and especially above Keokuk, gave a pilot sport enough without racing, and a captain had his keenest satisfaction in a punctually observed schedule. But there were occasional races—the twenty-two miles of broad clear water at Lake Pepin made a favorite racing ground—and the victorious steamboat proudly carried a broom, symbol of victory, on her pilothouse for a run or two.

However, one race on the Upper Mississippi became famous, a remarkable contest between two splendid boats and two storied captains. In 1856 the *Itasca*, under Captain David Whitten, and the *Grey Eagle*, under Captain Smith Harris, raced to St. Paul with copies of the message sent by Queen Victoria to President Buchanan inaugurating the Atlantic cable. The message had been flashed from the East over the new telegraph lines ending on the Mississippi at Dunleith and Prairie du Chien. At six o'clock that evening the *Itasca* started from Prairie du Chien for St. Paul, and at the same hour the *Grey Eagle* started north from the landing at Dunleith. The *Grey Eagle* had the longer run to make, by sixty-one miles; but she was the fastest boat on the Upper Mississippi and was out to make a record. She burned soft coal, and the firemen fed pitch into their furnace doors to keep the flames roaring. Grudgingly Captain Harris slowed down at the river landings to throw off mail; his intermediate freight he carried to St. Paul, planning to deliver it on the return trip. The *Itasca*, with sixty-one miles' start, made all the scheduled stops, but the stevedores set a record of their own as freight was hurried on board or hurled ashore.

The sixty-one miles looked like a big advantage at first, but steadily the *Eagle* narrowed it. At Lake Pepin the smoke of the *Itasca* was just fading over the water when the big boat entered the fairway. At Hastings, Captain Harris caught sight of the *Itasca.* From there on it was a frenzied race, with the boilers blowing, the tall stacks pouring columned smoke and the engines rocking. Just below St. Paul the *Grey Eagle* closed the distance and drew abreast. For a few moments the two boats swept through the river side by side, with the steam blowing from their safety valves and faces tense along their rails. Slowly the *Grey Eagle* pulled ahead. Ten feet, twenty, thirty—she was almost a length in front as they approached the levee. Captain Harris stood on his hurricane deck with the transatlantic message tied around a lump of coal. As he threw it ashore the crowded levee rang with cheers.

Both boats had set records for the run upriver. The *Grey Eagle* had come two hundred ninety miles from Dunleith in eighteen hours, and the *Itasca* had made two hundred twenty-nine miles from Prairie du Chien in the same time. Until the railroads linked St. Paul with the lower cities, those records stood unrivaled.

From the first appearance of steamers on the river, disaster was common. Since they carried steam they carried danger. Sensitive travelers considered high-pressure boats more dangerous than the others, and some of the slower boats made a boast of that feature, advertising "Low Pressure" in boxcar letters on their paddle casings. Charles Dickens, after a journey down the Ohio and up the Mississippi to St. Louis, wrote: "We had for ourselves a tiny stateroom opening out of the Ladies' Cabin. There was undoubtedly something satisfactory in this location, inasmuch as it was in the stern and we had been a great many times recommended to keep as far aft as possible because the steamboats generally blew up forward." Steamboat explosions were common enough, so that John Hay made it the chief virtue of his admirable Jim Bludso that when his boilers burst he would not leave his boat, but would

> . . . hold her nozzle agin the bank
> Till the last galoot's ashore.

After a long list of explosions, changes in steamboat inspection and in requirements of boiler construction reduced the disasters from overtaxed boilers.

But other hazards remained. Snags ripped open the bottom of many a well-built boat. Fires broke out in the wooden framing. Early in the season floating ice was a menace, and all season long there was the possibility of cyclones. The Mississippi drained a windy country; every year cyclonic storms struck somewhere on its upper reaches. They left wreckage behind them, and some good stories.

At midnight, while a gala Virgina reel was in progress in her cabin, a tornado struck the *Alexander Mitchell* of the Davidson Line. The wind came sudden and hard, before the pilot had a chance to seek the shelter of a lee shore. In a blinding, rending swoop it tore away both smokestacks and stripped the roof from the pilothouse. The mate was standing by the ship's bell when the blast came. Years afterward they said it picked him bodily off the deck and dropped him on shore a quarter of a mile away. The same account states that the port lifeboat was blown into a farmer's barnyard, a mile and a half across the prairie.

A curious, tragic sequence of disasters overtook the *Shepherdess* just three miles out of St. Louis in the winter of 1844. In the dark of night the boat struck a snag which opened her forward hull. Quickly the water rose to the boiler deck and passengers retreated to the topside. Amid clamor and confusion the boat's yawl was launched but as it filled with people the oars were lost from the rowlocks. A porter from the upper deck of the *Shepherdess* threw down a broom, and with that for a paddle the laden boat set out for shore. Meanwhile aboard the foundering steamer a young deck hand named Robert Bulloch went through scores of staterooms helping women and children to the hurricane deck. Among others he saved the "Ohio Fat Girl," a show woman of 440 pounds. Then the drifting *Shepherdess* struck a second snag. The lurch of that impact sent Robert Bulloch overboard, along with scores of others. He swam through numbing water to the Illinois shore. With the current pulling at her the steamer soon tore free from the snag and fetched up on the dark shore below St. Louis. Some people plunged into the water; others huddled on the tilting deck. At last the ferryboat *Icelander* arrived from St. Louis and took off the terrified survivors. Among the passengers on the doomed steamer had been a family of ten English immigrants. Five of them escaped to the Illinois side, four to the Missouri side, one was taken off by the ferry. They were all united in St. Louis. But seventy lives were lost from the *Shepherdess* that winter night.

The worst steamboat disaster on the Upper Mississippi occurred on the night of May 17, 1849, when fire swept the St. Louis water front. When the smoke cleared away from that famous levee, twenty-three steamers, three barges, and scores of smaller craft had been destroyed. Fire began at ten o'clock that night at the foot of Locust Street. There was never complete agreement on its cause, though a generally circulated report was that the fire began on the steamer *White Cloud*, where the steward had been airing his mattresses on deck while the craft lay at the landing. According to this account a spark from a passing steamer set fire to a mattress and the flames spread quickly, enveloping the boat and spreading both along the river and on shore. Fanned by a fresh spring wind the flames swept three blocks inland to Chestnut Street, and then crossed Chestnut at Commercial Alley. Changing direction, it burned from the alley to Main Street, and down Main Street to Market. By that time desperate firemen dynamited houses at Market and Second and checked the spread.

A large fleet of steamboats lay at the levee—the *White Cloud, Eudora, Edward Bates, Belle Isle, Julia,* and nearly twenty others. Almost as soon as the *White Cloud* took fire the wind carried the flames to the *Eudora* and the *Bates.* The *Bates* was either cut or burned loose from her moorings. She drifted along the levee, nudging other craft, spreading fire as she went. As the flames severed their mooring lines a blazing fleet drifted past the city. At last they fetched up on sand bars and burned out.

One result of that dreadful night was a new requirement on the riverboats. Rope hawsers were replaced with wire mooring cables that could not burn.

With dangers of wind and water, of channels and currents, and of the live steam in their own boilers, it is not strange that a steamboat's life was short. The pioneer steamer *Zebulon M. Pike* came up to St. Louis in 1817. By 1840 the *Pike*, number 8, and the *Ben Franklin*, number 7, were calling at St. Louis; all the earlier bearers of those names had been burned, exploded, broken up, or sunk. In less than forty years there were eight called *Post Boy* on the upper river. Five years, said George Byron Merrick, the famous Upper Mississippi pilot, was a good average life for a boat in those waters. Some never saw five years of service, and a few with a charmed life lasted twice that long. When George Merrick returned to St. Paul after fourteen years in the East, not a single vessel that he remembered remained on the river. The Upper Mississippi never had outmoded vessels, moored in retirement. Boats didn't grow old on that river.

But the greatest disaster that befell the steamboats was not nature's violence, the weakness of boiler plate, or the treachery of the channels. It was the coming of the railroads. In the winter of 1853-54 gangs of Irish workmen were grading the roadbed of the Mississippi and Missouri (now the Rock Island) Railroad. The first locomotive west of the Mississippi was ferried across to Davenport in 1854. When the gleaming rails reached the river in June of that year, a great excursion was arranged on the Mississippi as a celebration.

Five favorite steamboats had been chartered for a trip up the river. When the special train arrived at Rock

Island, the guests were transferred to spacious quarters in the *War Eagle, Galena, G. W. Sparrowhawk, Golden Era,* and *Lady Franklin.* The vessels glistened with fresh paint and polish. Aboard them was a distinguished company of 250 guests, including President Millard Fillmore, Charles A. Dana of the New York *Sun,* the historian George Bancroft, Mayor Isaac L. Millikin of Chicago, and a long list of notables from the United States Army, both houses of Congress, and financial circles of the East.

The river spectacle began with a display of fireworks, but to many an eastern visitor the burst of rockets in the sky was less impressive than the humped hills of the Mississippi, vague and portentous in the dark, with all the unpeopled West beyond them, and the mile-wide river murmuring beneath the stars. The excursion was designed to let men of influence see for themselves the vastness and grandeur of the valley. So the proud fleet made a landing at Dubuque and the party climbed at sunset to the high land where Julien Dubuque lies buried; from there they saw the evening darken over the river and the curving shores. The next day they visited Battle Island, where United States troops had driven Black Hawk's people into the river. They saw La Crosse and Trempeleau, and moored at sundown under Chimney Rock, the highest bluffs on the Mississippi. Next day the fleet steamed in line through the spacious waters of Lake Pepin, arriving at St. Paul in late afternoon. There they were banqueted in the House Chamber of the old capitol and heard the glories of the western country in a flow of western eloquence. When the excursion fleet was moored again at Rock Island, the pioneer western railroad sent men back to their desks and offices with a belief in the Mississippi country.

There is neat irony in the fact that steamboats provided a setting for the triumphant railroad celebration, because in a dozen years the railroads were to put an end to the steamboat's dominance in the valley. At first, as railheads reached the river, the boats received an increased trade; in the late fifties there were not vessels enough to carry the goods and passengers waiting at the landings. But when the railroads crossed the river, and reached north along its shores, the golden age of steamboating was over.

It was not long after that fine excursion that the bitter and losing rivalry began. Across the river at Davenport the Rock Island Railroad built a wooden bridge, with five spans and a center draw. The first train crossed over on April 22, 1856. Two weeks later, on May 6th, the packet boat *Effie Alton* failed to pass through the draw successfully. As she neared the bridge the current caught her. One of her paddles stopped, for some unaccounted reason, and she swung against a central pier. With the impact her galley stove tipped over, setting fire to the boat. While she lay there burning, the wooden bridge took fire. No more trains crossed to Iowa that year.

Then the recriminations began. The *Effie Alton's* pilot was charged with deliberately wrecking his vessel so as to destroy the bridge. But the steamboat company sued the railroad for damages. Popular sentiment favored the steamboats; they were well-established in the country and had become a part of the frontier life. The railroad directors needed the service of a shrewd and persuasive lawyer. After careful search they chose a frontier lawyer from Sangamon County, Illinois—"one of the best to state a case forcibly and convincingly, with a personality to appeal to any judge and jury hereabouts." He was Abe Lincoln.

The ensuing case ended in compromise. Future bridge laws were designed to guard against the obstruction of navigation on the river, and steamboatmen agreed to modify the height of their smokestacks so that they could pass under the bridges that were to stride at many places across the Mississippi.

CHAPTER 14

Men of the Mississippi

As it was men more than machines that triumphed over the upper river's shoals, bars and currents, so it was men who added most to the accumulating lore of the steamboat age. All the stories of the river's hazards and the trade's excitement are dominated by men. Their names have been remembered long after their boats foundered or were broken up. The river was a hard school and it produced salty, vigorous, original men.

There are many vanished captains whose names retain a living freshness. Captain Asa Green, master and owner of the *Equator*, which was wrecked at the mouth of the St. Croix in 1858, was a fervent, hymn-singing, gospel-quoting man. Tom Cushing, pilot and captain, took up steamboating after a career as an opera singer in New York; from his hurricane deck he sang heroic arias at midnight, testing the acoustics of the bluff-framed valley. Captain William H. Laughton, an Englishman by birth, became famous for feats of lifesaving; nine times he leaped fully clothed over the rail for people who had fallen overboard. Captain John B. Davis, master of a big boat at nineteen years of age, won reputation as a shoal-water man, having great skill at taking a boat over sunken bars and ridges. He finally left the Mississippi for the shallower channels of the Missouri, and while commanding the *Freighter* in a spring flood he tried a short cut, crossing a stretch of inundated land between Big Stone Lake and the Red River of the North. He got along pretty well for a couple of hours, but then he grounded on the prairie and was wrecked ten miles from his proper channel. Captain David Tipton had perhaps the longest career of all Upper Mississippi steamboatmen; after sixty years of piloting he dropped dead at his wheel at the age of eighty-four. Count Ageston Haraszthy, a political refugee from Hungary, bought the small steamer *Rock River,* and in the dignity of his stovepipe hat commanded her for a few runs between the Fever River and Mendota. A scholarly and aristocratic Englishman, Robert C. Eden, bought an eighty-ton side-wheeler, filled her cabin with books and cruised the Upper Mississippi, Wisconsin, and St. Croix rivers. Captain William F. Davidson was a teetotaler who permitted no drinking, gambling, or dancing on his boats. He built a fleet of vessels and had their cabins decorated with large dramatic murals depicting the evils of strong drink.

It is a rich gallery to choose from, but there is good reason to name two steamboatmen from all the rest and to believe that they will longest be remembered on the river. I give you Daniel Smith Harris, the Fighting Skipper, and George Byron Merrick, pilot and river historian, who already has a State Park named for him.

At Galena in 1823, when the lead diggings were still primitive scratches on the hillsides, a fifteen-year-old boy, Daniel Smith Harris, arrived with his parents and four brothers on a keelboat from the Ohio. A few weeks later the gangling boy watched the historic *Vir-*

ginia steam triumphantly up the Mississippi. He did not know it then, but as he watched the churning paddle-wheels and the smoking stacks he was looking at his own future. Within a few years the Harris brothers had assembled a steam engine and installed it in the *Jo Daviess,* the first of a line of steamboats which they built at Galena. Through the great decades of the forties and fifties Daniel Smith Harris took the lead in the construction of Upper Mississippi vessels and he became the most famous steamboatman on the river. He hung up many speed records and unceasingly improved the design of his boats, setting a pace and a standard that were the despair of all his rivals. He was a showman who never lost the love of display nor the flair for surrounding his boats with novelty and drama. From the early *Smelter,* which he decorated with evergreens and mounted with a cannon to announce her progress and arrival, to his masterpiece, the *Grey Eagle,* the biggest, finest, and fastest boat on the upper river, his steamers led the way.

He was also a skilled pilot and a desperate racer. While he commanded the *Senator,* the *Dr. Franklin,* number 2, the *Nominee,* the *Louella,* the *New St. Paul,* the *West Newton,* and the *War Eagle,* he was rarely passed on the river. Rival masters and pilots never sought a brush with him. He had a furious temper, a purple vocabulary, and a burning pride in every boat he owned or commanded.

His final boat, the *Grey Eagle,* brought him his greatest triumph. Built in 1857 at a cost of $63,000, she was the last word in size, efficiency, and refinement on the Upper Mississippi. In the *Grey Eagle* Captain

Harris made his record run, beating the *Itasca* to St. Paul with the historic cable message. But her life was short. In 1861, while he stood in the pilothouse, his fine boat struck the Rock Island bridge, colliding square amidships in a hard current. It took her just five minutes to sink. After that Captain Harris retired from the river, watching the dwindling commerce from his home in Galena, growing old beside the waters that had set their spell on him in his boyhood.

George Byron Merrick is the Mark Twain of the Upper Mississippi. He first saw the river at Rock Island, as a twelve-year-old boy, on a summer day in 1854. Being fascinated by the steamer *Louella*, with her stern wheel idly revolving in the current, he was told by a joking bystander that the craft was not a steamboat at all but a water-power sawmill. It was not many years before George Merrick knew every vessel on the river.

At the mouth of the St. Croix River stood the frontier settlement of Prescott, Wisconsin, and here, among two hundred white people and five hundred Indians, George Merrick spent an enthralling boyhood. There were many things to wonder at—the Indians, the forest and the prairie, the memories of fur traders and military outposts, and the still living mystery of the wilderness. But what held the most excitement was the wide-curving Mississippi and the steamboats that came and went around its bends. The Merrick family lived in the upper portion of a warehouse fronting the river, his father's freight business occupying the lower part. There George Merrick and his brother became "levee rats." They haunted the river at all seasons and they never missed, at any hour of the day or night, a steamboat landing at their levee. "Was she a side-wheel or stern-wheel? Was she large or small? Had she trimmings on her smokestack, or about the pilot house, and if so of what description? Had she a 'Texas' or no 'Texas'? Were the outside blinds painted white, red, or green? What was the sound of her whistle and bell? All of these points, and many others, were taken in, and indelibly impressed upon our memories, so that if the whistle or bell were again heard, perhaps months afterward, the name of the boat could be given with almost unfailing accuracy." This was the heart and soul of George Merrick's education. It was inevitable that he should go on the river. An apprenticeship as a printer fitted into the winter season, after the close of navigation, but when the boats were running George Merrick could not stand quiet at a case of type. He began his river career as a pantry boy, on the *Kate Cassell*. Then he was "cub" engineer, mud-clerk (whose duty it was to go out in all weather on the unpaved levees to check the discharge and delivery of freight), and eventually pilot of some of the storied boats on the river. In those years he learned all the men and traditions of the Upper Mississippi. He piloted Dan Rice's circus boat to pioneer towns on the Mississippi and its tributaries. He piloted Major Bob Eden's *Enterprise* for a blissful season to the hunting and fishing grounds of Wisconsin, and in the tranquil evenings he traded stories of the Mississippi for the English gentleman's accounts of Oxford, London, Paris, and Berlin. There was nothing provincial about life on the Upper Mississippi.

The Civil War ended George Merrick's career on the river. After the war he became a steamship agent and superintendent in New York, and it was years before he looked again on the Mississippi. When he returned he found half a dozen railroads centering in St. Paul, doing the business of the hundreds of steamboats he had left running in 1862. Now, in the middle seventies, a dozen boats, belonging to just two remaining lines, were handling all the river business between St. Paul and St. Louis, and the profession of piloting was at an end.

But the great years on the river had not vanished from George Merrick's memory. With the later perspective of time and a kindling warmth of recollection, he wrote *Old Times on the Upper Mississippi*, a book that will keep the names of Tom Cushing and Tom Burns, of Smith Harris and Bob Eden alive for many generations. And after George Merrick's death a commanding stretch of Mississippi River bluffs above Fountain City, Wisconsin, was made public property and named in his honor. Now Merrick State Park is one of the landmarks of the valley.

CHAPTER 15

The Mammoth Panoramas

THE Mississippi moved men's imaginations. In the middle years of the last century the river was the most dramatic scene in America, with the full tide of western commerce on its waters and the activity of the frontier along its shores. The river was a boundary, the end of the possessed land and the beginning of the unpossessed; the sun set over the bluffs of Iowa and Minnesota in a heroic light. It is not strange, then, that the Mississippi inspired artists like George Catlin and Seth Eastman to paint its varied scenes of wilderness and civilization. And it is not strange that other artists, less gifted and less disciplined, felt its spell. So the painters of the mammoth panoramas, one of them "four miles long," put the pageant of the river on canvas.

The Mississippi existed on a vast scale, and the panoramists undertook to emulate it. They weren't content to select Trempeleau Mountain or the vista of Lake Pepin; they wanted the whole sweep and variety of the river. The Mississippi was the largest river known to civilized man; they set to work on the largest paintings ever attempted. It was logical, at least.

The curious thing is that the panoramas were all products of a single decade, perhaps the most dramatic decade on the upper river, when the elemental wilderness was still vying with the civilization that was to supplant it. Between 1840 and 1850 six painters recorded the Mississippi on canvas panoramas from four hundred yards to four miles long. Such paintings could be viewed, like the river itself, only part at a time. They were unrolled before audiences, as the valley unrolled from the deck of a steamboat, and they were seen by hundreds of thousands of marveling spectators in America and Europe. The name and the marvels of the Mississippi had become known around the earth. There was no lack of patronage for the panoramas.

The first one was the work of a St. Louis scene painter who tired of the limitations of his trade. John Rawson Smith painted a river sequence which after a few exhibitions was destroyed by fire. Thereupon he painted a bigger and better one, four miles long, according to one account, and took it on tour through the United States. After a long domestic tour he took it abroad, in 1848, showing it in England and on the Continent for several seasons more. His painting depicted in a series of scenes the entire valley, from the Falls of St. Anthony to the Gulf of Mexico.

Another St. Louis man who felt the drama of the river and was moved to put it onto canvas was John Banvard, proprietor of a museum which may have grown tame and tedious to him. Resolved to make the largest painting in the world, he undertook a leisurely journey down the river, sketching as he went. When he had his sketches made he settled down to a patient job of painting on huge rolls of canvas twelve feet high. His finished panorama was said to measure an even three miles. This picture he displayed to nearly half a million Americans, in all the principal cities, and in 1848 he took it across the Atlantic. In England his exhibit scored an enormous success. It ran for twenty months of daily showings at London's Egyptian Hall and was shown by royal command to Queen Victoria in Windsor Castle. Before his return to America, John Banvard took his display to Paris, where it showed with almost equal success.

At least four other Mississippi panoramas were painted in the late 1840's, all of them by St. Louis artists. That the projects of Smith and Banvard had proved financially lucrative accounts in part for this curious burst of artistic effort; the dramatic appeal of the river and its fascination for people far and near must make up the remaining explanation. Of the several panoramas, a comparatively modest one by Leon Pomarede, not quite two thousand feet in length, was the most novel and striking. It was concerned entirely with the upper portions of the river and featured scenes from Indian life. War dances, buffalo hunts, dog feasts, and a raging prairie fire were portrayed in brilliant colors, while other scenes depicted Indian villages on the riverbanks and Indian canoes carrying furs to the trading posts. The river commerce was dramatically represented by "Mechanical Moving Figures of Steamboats" in which, by a mechanical arrangement behind the canvas, smoke was made to pour out of the upright stacks and the audience heard the unmistakable hissing of pent-up steam. The Pomarede panorama ended climactically with a "beautiful dissolving view of the Great Fire at St. Louis." In this sequence the artist represented the holocaust in all its fury, the flames leaping under a crimson-tinted sky and people fleeing from the destruction of their city.

As the panorama unrolled and daylight appeared, the Mississippi was pictured "gorged with the half-sunken wrecks and charred remains of twenty-three steamers," and acres of the city were a smoking ruin.

The most famous of the panoramas was the work of a more sober artist, who spared no pains to make his work educational as well as awe-inspiring, and who prided himself on its fidelity. Henry Lewis, an Englishman, went to St. Louis in 1836, where he became a stage carpenter in Ben De Bar's Opera House. He was a self-taught artist, with a carpenter's good sense of building lines; the contours of his landscapes and the lines of his houses are better done than the animated figures which appear in his Mississippi scenes. When the idea came to him to paint a panorama he prepared methodically for the task. In June of 1848 he left St. Louis for a careful tour of the upper river, to select the scenes and make preliminary sketches. On the steamboat *Senator* he journeyed to Fort Snelling, enjoying the company of Henry Hastings Sibley, a fellow passenger, who told him stories of the Indians and of the western hunting grounds that must have helped to prepare Lewis for the painting of his primitive scenes on the upper reaches of the river.

Lewis's plan was to float downstream from Fort Snelling, stopping to explore tributaries, to survey the landscape, and to make abundant sketches that would be the basis of his panorama. At Fort Snelling he bought two extremely long canoes and some sawed lumber. These materials he combined into the oddest craft ever launched upon the Mississippi. His canoes were fifty feet long with steeply upturned ends; he used them, in tandem, three feet apart, as a double-keel for a raftlike platform on which he erected a cabin eight by eleven feet. A rough-hewn mast was rigged with foresail and jib. After loading provisions and supplies he was ready for his journey. "It made a Boat admirably adapted to my purpose as it was *quite steady* and from the top of my Cabin, I could sketch with care and see over the Country on both sides of the River." This grotesque and useful craft he named the *Minnehaha*, painting the name in big bright letters on the sides of the cabin. He took pains to include the "littel Boat" in a couple of his paintings. Consequently, its appearance has been preserved though the *Minnehaha* was destroyed, along with a score of bigger and less distinctive craft in the great riverfront fire at St. Louis in the following spring.

The long, leisurely voyage in the *Minnehaha* proved, though marred by some discomforts, to be marked by many carefree hours, many convivial meetings, and a sense of almost constant delight. With Lewis was his collaborator, John S. Robb of St. Louis, a printer by trade, who was to write a commentary to accompany the panorama. They were excellent traveling companions, sharing both pleasures and troubles with good spirit.

The troubles began the first night out from Fort Snelling. As Henry Lewis puts it in his journal of the voyage, it was "a trouble which although it may appear very insignificant at first sight threatens to rob us of half the pleasure of our trip, if not half our blood. I mean the musquetoes. I had often heard people talk of clouds of these tormentors and of persons being eaten alive. These I considered figurative expressions, but sorry experience has taught me that they are too true. Had we remain'd expos'd to their attacks in the bottom in which we encamped that night all that would have been left of the chronicler of this journal would have been his skeliton."

The next day they rigged a mosquito bar entirely around the cabin and Lewis made a few sketches, not, however, without distraction:

> Altogether it was a wretched day and we hail'd with pleasure a beautiful looking spot about ½ past 7 where we concluded we would encamp. But oh how appearances in nature as well as in man do sometimes deceive. This you would suppose the breading place of all the blooded stock of this most blood thirsty crew. We had hardly landed when we were attacked by hundreds. The fire after it was made attracted thousands and we ate our supper attended by the obsequious attentions of millions, until fairly driven into our tent and under our own bar where we thought we should have some little peace. But bars were no bar to them and we had scarsely got under it when whiz whiz, hum hum you would have thought yourself in a hive of bees. It was dreadful after the fatigue and heat of the day thus to be anoy'd so we determin'd if possible to kill every one in the bar and then try and sleep again so procuring a light we went to work and kill'd some hundreds and once more compos'd our selves but it was no use—in they came again I don't know how, for the bar was perfect, and we got no sleep that night and were fairly driven away without our breakfast, for it was impossible to eat it even if we cook'd it.

But there were other, more welcome visitors to the *Minnehaha*. Frequently a band of Indians smelled the

supper on their fire and came to call. They made cere-
monious speeches, complimenting the travelers and their
wonderful boat, and ended by begging bread. And there
were occasional visits from settlers along the shores,
curious about the *Minnehaha* and anxious to look over
Lewis's shoulder as he made his drawings.

The Mississippi moved Lewis genuinely. In squalls
of wind and rain or in the windless amber sunset, from
the heights of Mount Trempeleau or in the lush Bad
Axe bottom lands, he felt the many moods of the river
and its aloof elemental power. "Yet a feeling of sadness
would break over one to think that all this beauty—
this adaptation of nature's to man's wants was a *solitude,*
vast, and lonely, and inhabited only by a few bands of
Indians now fast melting away and the solitary deer and
elk. No smoke from the cabin to remind one of home
and its comforts, no spires, or domes of cities to tell of
commerce or its manufacturies, no waving fields of grain
to contrast with its golden undulations the vast masses
of dark green foliage. . . . As I looked I felt how hopeless art was to convey the *soul* of such a scene." In his
paintings Lewis did suggest the elemental quality of the
great valley; the lights and shadows on the shores, the
high arched sky and the solemn flowing river.

Frequently they stopped half a day to hunt, tramping through the forest with their rifles ready. At a pleasant camping site they lingered long enough to roast fish
in the coals and to bake loaves of bread. They left their
names, like schoolboys, carved on a tree trunk or painted
on the rocks in Lewis's bold brush strokes. In the evening, while Lewis put finishing touches on the day's
drawings, his companion stretched out in a bunk and
read Dicken's newest novel, *Dombey and Son;* then they

lit their pipes and talked while the katydids chorused from the shore and the river murmured around them. So they made a pleasant journey, full of discovery and delight, between the changing shores. When they passed rafts and flatboats, rivermen stared curiously and sang out "What you got to sell, stranger?" The *Minnehaha* did look like a floating vendor's stand, and Lewis answered without a moment's hesitation, "Elephant's tusks!" or "Carcassian slaves!" or something else that left the raftsmen muttering to each other.

Below Galena, in the populous central valley, they stopped often, as Lewis wanted to include a sketch of every town and settlement; his panorama was to be both accurate and complete. At Nauvoo they visited the Mormon Temple, making careful drawings of it, and called on the widow of Joseph Smith. At Clarksville they camped under a tree thirty-four feet in girth. There Lewis was impressed by the grandeur of the forest and the wan and shaking children in the Illinois town where ague was as common and recurrent as summer. He made a sketch of the mouth of the Illinois River and several others of the palisades along the shore to Alton. On August 4, 1848, one month after the *Minnehaha* had steered into the stream at Fort Snelling, he made his final sketch, of the mouth of the Missouri, and the *Minnehaha* came to rest at the St. Louis levee.

That winter Lewis worked feverishly at a great roll of canvas twenty-five hundred feet long and twelve feet high, painting the more important scenes himself and directing the work of several assistants. In the autumn of 1849 his panorama showed in St. Louis, with special matinees for school children. After several weeks there, he took it to the eastern cities. In Washington it was viewed in the White House by President Zachary Taylor and a party of government officials. President Taylor, who had served for years at army posts on the Upper Mississippi, must have found the scenes rich in memory and association.

To England and the Continent Lewis went with his exhibit. In Germany he found enormous interest in the Mississippi, as the Revolution of 1848 had already caused a great German emigration to the river valley. In Düsseldorf he contracted for the publication of a book depicting the Mississippi country in words and in colored lithographic plates. The resulting *Das illustrierte Mississippithal* was an impressive book, but shortly after its appearance the publishers failed and the unbound copies of the work were sold as waste paper. Only a few copies of the book were preserved, and it was for a number of years a rare and valuable title. However, in 1923 the book was reprinted.

Lewis did not return to America but lived on in Germany, serving for a time as United States consular agent at Düsseldorf and studying and practicing art until his death in 1904. In his final years he turned to the Mississippi sketches he had made half a century before and painted several Upper Mississippi views which now hang in galleries in Minneapolis and St. Paul.

The Lewis panorama, like all the others, has disappeared. It was reported to have been bought by an Englishman and taken to India. There in vagueness and uncertainty ends the story of the panorama that brought to hundreds of thousands who had never seen the Mississippi a sense of the great river flowing through the heart of North America.

CHAPTER 16

Enchanted Boyhood

HANNIBAL, MISSOURI, is a railroad town, with a certain fame as a pioneer railhead on the far side of the Mississippi; in 1856 its first train ran west over the raw new roadbed into the unshaped West. In Hannibal's shops railroadmen put together the first mail car in the world, and there in the year of Appomattox was built the famous General Grant, the first locomotive constructed west of the Mississippi.

This is an odd quirk of history, because Hannibal has another kind of fame which makes it forever a drowsing sunlit town where the vanished steamboats ply the river and where two barefoot boys tramp immortally through the dusty streets with fishing poles on their shoulders. They stand there now, two figures in bronze at the foot of Cardiff Hill, barefoot and in tattered clothes, and they are looking toward the river. A few miles away, in a straggling Misouri village, Mark Twain was born when all that country was waiting for the future. He became a part of its future, and as artist and philosopher he gave the Mississippi to the world. So Tom Sawyer still slides down the back roof to keep a rendezvous with Huckleberry Finn, and they are off on immortal errands through the moonlit alleys and the meadows drenched in dew. The steamers that called at Hannibal's landing are gone to oblivion and long ago the General Grant rusted down to scrap iron. But St. Petersburg and Jackson's Island, McDowell's Cave and Cardiff Hill, and a raft floating past the changing Mississippi shores have become a part of boyhood everywhere.

When Mark Twain lived in Hannibal it was a tranquil town on the edge of settlement. The great river ran in grandeur between the bluffs of Missouri and the forests of Illinois. Here was a country unhurried, largely unpossessed, keeping its carelessness and beauty a little longer. It was this way that Mark Twain remembered it all his life long:

> . . . the white town drowsing in the sunshine of a summer's morning; the streets empty, or pretty nearly so; one or two clerks sitting in front of the Water Street stores, with their splint-bottomed chairs tilted back against the walls, chins on breasts, hats slouched over their faces, asleep—with shingle-shavings enough around to show what broke them down; a sow and a litter of pigs loafing along the sidewalk, doing a good business in watermelon rinds and seeds, two or three lonely little freight piles scattered about the "levee"; a pile of "skids" on the slope of the stone-paved wharf, and the fragrant town drunkard asleep in the shadow of them; two or three wood flats at the head of the wharf, but nobody to listen to the peaceful lapping of the wavelets against them; the great Mississippi, the majestic, the magnificent Mississippi, rolling its mile-wide tide along, shining in the sun; the dense forest away on the other side; the "point" above the town, and the "point" below, bounding the river-

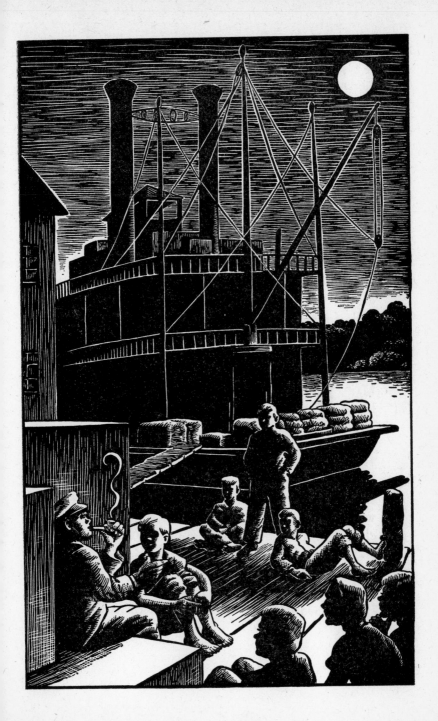

glimpse and turning it into a sort of sea, and withal a very still and brilliant and lovely one.

Sitting in the village schoolroom young Sam Clemens could look off to the heights of Halliday's Hill and Lover's Leap; his mind could be over the hills and far away. There were windy ridges where a boy could feel close to the sky and deep wooded glens that always kept a forest twilight. Flowing down to the river were secluded little tributaries, like Bear Creek, with deep clear swimming holes. Out in the Mississippi were long islands of wilderness, Turtle Island and Glasscock's Island, where boys could live like Indians or pirates. In a rank field at the edge of town was a deserted house, full of fear and wonder, and it was rumored that somewhere on the riverbank a French trapper had buried a chest of gold. There were steamboats at the landing and men telling river stories in the long summer evenings. Many years later, on a soft warm night in India when his thoughts went back to the Mississippi, Mark Twain wrote: "All that goes to make the *me* in me was in a Missouri village on the other side of the globe."

Three miles down the river, on the steep, brush-covered hillside, was the mysterious entry into Mc-Dowell's Cave. No one had explored all its labyrinthine windings. There were secret passages and marvelous chambers that no one had seen, not even the St. Louis doctor who had placed a girl's body in a remote cleft, fretted with stalactites, to see if it would petrify. The dark corridors ran far back under the bluffs, too far even for the bats to find their way, and there were reports that some passages led down under the Mississippi. A boy's imagination could never exhaust the marvelous world that opened like a bear's den in the hillside.

Everybody in Hannibal knew everybody else in a neighborly sort of way. But it was not a drab and uniform society. There were people of good family—this was essentially a southern town and social lines were very clear. There were people without family, and they knew that no pretense could make good that lack. What was more satisfying to a boy was the third element, the riffraff of the town—vagrant rivermen, transient raftsmen, half-civilized holdovers from the age before like the dissolute Injun Joe, and the harmless drunkards, General Gaines and Jimmy Finn, and old Ben Blankenship who gave a son to the world's literature—Tom Blankenship was the ragamuffin who rafted to immortality as Huckleberry Finn. There was, too, another element, perhaps the most human and haunting of all. Hannibal was a slave town and so it had its Negroes. As a boy Mark Twain heard them tell their strange and childish stories, he heard them sing the homesick plantation melodies, he saw them solemnly observe their superstitions. He never forgot a syllable of their sorrow and their wonder.

Every summer in his early boyhood Mark Twain spent a few weeks at the farm of his uncle, John Quarles, a few miles back in the wooded Missouri country. Here was a rich, roomy rural life. There were eight children in the Quarles household, and fifteen or twenty Negroes. Mark Twain remembered it sharply, poignantly, for fifty years:

It was a heavenly place for a boy, that farm of my Uncle John's. The house was a double long one, with a spacious floor (roofed in) connecting it with the kitchen. In the summer the table was set in the middle of that shady and breezy floor, and the sumptuous meals—well, it makes me cry to think of them. Fried chicken, roast pig; wild and tame turkeys, ducks and geese; venison just killed; squirrels, rabbits, pheasants, partridges, prairie-chickens; biscuits, hot batter cakes, hot buckwheat cakes, hot "wheat bread," hot rolls, hot corn pone; fresh corn boiled on the ear, succotash, butter-beans, string-beans; tomatoes, peas, Irish potatoes, sweet potatoes; buttermilk, sweet milk, "clabber"; watermelons, musk-melons, cantaloupes—all fresh from the garden; apple pie, peach pie, pumpkin pie, apple dumplings, peach cobbler—I can't remember the rest.

It was a place as rich for the spirit as for a boy's sharp appetite. In a storied old city by the Danube Mark Twain wrote in 1898:

I can call back the solemn twilight and mystery of the deep woods, the earthly smells, the faint odors of the wild flowers, the sheen of rain-washed foliage, the rattling clatter of drops when the wind shook the trees, the far-off hammering of woodpeckers and the muffled drumming of wood pheasants in the remoteness of the forest, the snapshot pictures of disturbed wild creatures scurrying through the grass—I can call it all back and make it as real as it ever was, and as blessed.

This was a life that never faded in his memory; rather it deepended and intensified and became the background for his storytelling:

I remember the 'coon and 'possum hunts, nights, with the negroes, and the long marches through the black gloom of the woods, and the excitement which fired everybody when the distant bay of an experienced dog announced that the game was treed; then the wild scramblings and stumblings through briers and bushes and over roots to get to the spot; then the lighting of the fire and the felling of the tree, the joyful frenzy of the dogs and the negroes, and the weird picture it all made in the red glare—I remember it all well, and the delight that everybody got out of it, except the 'coon.

I remember the pigeon seasons, when the birds would come in millions and cover the trees and by their weight break down the branches. They were clubbed to death with sticks; guns were not necessary and were not used. I remember the squirrel hunts and prairie-chicken hunts, and wild-turkey hunts, and all that; and how we turned out, mornings, when it was still dark, to go on these expeditions, and how chilly and dismal it was, and how often I regretted that I was well enough to go. A toot on a tin horn brought twice as many dogs as were needed, and in their happiness they raced and scampered about, and knocked small people down, and made no end of unnecessary noise. At the word, they vanished away toward the woods, and we drifted silently after them in the melancholy gloom. But presently the gray dawn stole over the world, the birds piped up, then the sun rose and poured light and comfort all around, everything was fresh and dewy and fragrant and life was a boon again.

But it was the Mississippi moving past the streets of Hannibal that provided pure enchantment. Without the river it would have been a backwoods boyhood, full of wildness and freedom; with the river it had another quality, a horizon, the moving power of beauty, and the tug at the imagination. The unpeopled woods and the sparsely settled prairies were evidence of the town's isolation; they hemmed a frontier settlement in. But the river was a way out. A marvelous commerce passed the doors of Hannibal, long rafts that came from the pineries of the north, scows and flatboats from the trading stations, steamboats from the cities down below.

In such a town every boy knew the steamboats, from the first glimpse as they came smoking round the bend. In fact he knew them without ever seeing the tall stacks and the gleaming texas; he knew a boat by its whistle's pitch and the sound of its bells. And he knew where it came from, what cargo it carried, and where it was bound. Usually he knew the captain's name and what pilot was aboard.

No boy could be provincial, letting a small world close about him, while he lived beside the river. With all its moods, mysterious with moonlight and gemmed with stars, vast with autumn fog and sullen with the flooding waters of April, it was changeless and yet ever changing. It was inexhaustible. A boy could breast its strong current, striking out for the green islands or even across to the distant Illinois shore. He could steal a skiff and play pirate; he could be a fisherman, an outlaw, a steamboatman. And when adventure was not enough there was the river to follow in his mind, to places he had never looked upon or heard of in the drawling talk of Missouri people.

Long before he became a pilot Mark Twain made his first voyages. When he was nine years old he stowed away on a big packet, going aboard at Hannibal and hiding beneath a lifeboat on the upper deck. When the bell clanged and the paddle wheel rumbled he crept out of his dark corner and stared with wide eyes at the hurrying water and the passing shores. The pound of the engines came to him and the great soft thresh of the paddlewheel. He was on a steamboat, bound downriver. They found him and put him ashore—at Louisiana. It was not the Louisiana of cottonfields and bayous, it was the quiet town of Louisiana, Missouri, just nine miles below Hannibal. He had an uncle in that town, who took him back to Hannibal where his father waited sternly. But the stars were still in his eyes.

Even when he had learned the river with all the weary, memory-racking knowledge of a pilot, he never lost a sense of the river's grandeur and mystery. He knew every mile of it between St. Louis and New Orleans, every bend and bar, every town and landing, but it never became routine or empty to him. Years later, for the great tale of boyhood in America, he sent Huck Finn drifting down those waters on a raft. And Huck tells us how daylight came over the great river:

> Two or three days and nights went by; I reckon I might say they swum by, they slid along so quiet and smooth and lovely. Here is the way we put in the time. It was a monstrous big river down there—sometimes a mile and a half wide; we

run nights, and laid up and hid day-times; soon as night was almost gone, we stopped navigating and tied up—nearly always in the dead water under a tow-head; and then cut young cottonwoods and willows and hid the raft with them. Then we set out the lines. Next we slid into the river and had a swim, so as to freshen up and cool off; then we set down on the sandy bottom where the water was about knee deep, and watched the daylight come. Not a sound, anywheres—perfectly still—just like the whole world was asleep, only sometimes the bull-frogs a-cluttering maybe. The first thing to see, looking away over the water, was a kind of dull line—that was the woods on t'other side—you couldn't make nothing else out; then a pale place in the sky; then more paleness, spreading around; then the river softened up, away off, and warn't black any more, but gray; you could see little dark spots drifting along, ever so far away—trading scows and such things; and long black streaks—rafts; sometimes you could hear a sweep screaking; or jumbled up voices, it was so still, and sounds come so far; and by-and-by you could see a streak on the water which you know by the look of the streak that there's a snag there in a swift current which breaks on it and makes that streak look that way; and you see the mist curl up off of the water, and the east reddens up, and the river, and you make out a log cabin in the edge of the woods, away on the bank on t'other side of the river, being a wood-yard, likely, and piled by them cheats so you can throw a dog through it anywheres; then the nice breeze springs up, and comes fanning you from over there, so cool and fresh, and sweet to smell, on account of the woods and the flowers; but some-

times not that way because they've left dead fish
laying around, gars, and such, and they do get
pretty rank; and next you've got the full day, and
everything smiling in the sun, and the song-birds
just going it!

A little smoke could be noticed, now, so we
would take some fish off of the lines, and cook up
a hot breakfast. And afterwards we would watch
the lonesomeness of the river, and kind of lazy
along, and by-and-by lazy off to sleep. Wake up,
by-and-by, and look to see what done it, and maybe
see a steamboat, coughing along up stream, so far
off towards the other side you couldn't tell nothing
about her only whether she was stern-wheel or side-
wheel; then for about an hour there wouldn't be
nothing to hear nor nothing to see—just solid lonesomeness. Next you'd see a raft sliding by, away off
yonder, and maybe a galoot on it chopping, because
they're most always doing it on a raft; you'd see the
ax flash, and come down—you don't hear nothing;
you see that ax go up again, and by the time it's
above the man's head, then you hear the *k'chunk!*
—it had took all that time to come over the water.
So we would put in the day, lazying around, listening to the stillness.

Now that we have Mark Twain, the boy growing
up beside the river, the pilot taking the big steamboats
on the long run, the novelist telling the stories of the
great years on the Mississippi, it seems inevitable that
the river should have produced its interpreter. No other
of the earth's rivers is so intermingled with a man's life,
but here the two are inseparable. The river gave Sam
Clemens the name the world was to know him by, and
he gave the river its place in the stories that men cherish.

PART THREE

The Epic of Lumber

CHAPTER 17

Woods to the World's End

"WOODS to the world's end!"

So Solomon Juneau in his log hut at Milwaukee had answered Cleng Peerson's question, "What lies to the north?"

The great enterprise of the Middle Border, dwarfing all others in its drama and riches, was the cutting of the northern forests. And there Cleng Peerson's men were to come with axes and peaveys, raising the cry *Timber-r-r!* in the instant before a giant pine thundered to the ground.

From early times men had known the vastness of the pine woods. Radisson and Groseilliers had tramped on snowshoes through frozen tamarack swamps and endless tracts of pine. The early reports of government surveyors show men baffled by "one immense pine forest" four hundred miles square. Follow the 44th parallel across Wisconsin from Lake Michigan to the Mississippi at La Crosse. Draw lines north all the way to Sault Ste. Marie and the Lake of the Woods. See every acre of that empire clothed in pine and spruce and tamarack. From the quiet bend of the Wisconsin River to the roar of International Falls, see the little streams all flowing through a twilight and hear the wind soughing in dark branches. Here is a country as big as France. And it was all woods. If not to the world's end, then far beyond the limits of surveyors' ranges in the time of Solomon Juneau.

Logging began on the Upper Mississippi before the land was open to timber claims or settlement. In 1823 when Fort Snelling was building the government set up a sawmill, where now the big flour mills rise above St. Anthony's Falls, for the manufacture of lumber to supply the fort. Seeing the promise of future wealth, several of the fort's first officers squatted on claims from which they proposed to control the water power of the Falls. When, twenty years later, the settlement was legalized, Franklin Steele had the most strategic site. He plotted the village of St. Anthony and built a commercial sawmill, and lumbering began.

In those years at many places in the Upper Mississippi valley men were choosing homesteads near timber and water. Settlers of the edge of the pineries felled the timber on their claims and hauled it to the first crude mills. When Wisconsin pine found a market in the growing towns along the Mississippi, the first logging camps were established up the northern rivers. These were small outfits of a dozen men who lived in low dark shanties lighted by the open fire where the cook swung his red-hot kettles over the burning logs. Some of their first recruits were the Norse settlers who in their native land had been lumbermen as well as farmers. Big Ole Olsen and Gunder Skistad were ready to leave their snowbound fields for a winter's job in the deep woods. They looked a lot like pine trunks themselves, solid and dark against the snow.

There were other races in the camps, Maine men with Scotch and Irish names, and French Canadians who

had already logged on the Ottawa and the Saginaw as the industry moved west along the St. Lawrence and the Great Lakes. But in the Mississippi forests the Scandinavian woodsman became the dominant figure. As time passed, the Swedes, Norwegians, Danes, and Finns came in increasing numbers to the camps; it was Big Ole and Happy Olsen and Chris Crosshaulson who became the immortals of Paul Bunyan's crew.

In the early camps men did the work by hand, with the aid of instruments which Maine loggers had brought to the West—the go-devil, the ax, and the peavey. There were no railroads to haul the cut to the mills. But the pine stood thick on the banks of streams, and it was a short haul for the oxen to drag the logs through brush and snow to a steep place on the riverbank. There they waited for the spring water to carry them down to the bull ponds and the booming yards.

The first steamboat to find her way to the richly timbered valley of the St. Croix River was the *Palmyra*. In the summer of 1839 she trailed her plume of smoke between the forest shores. She was met by a hungry and impatient band of Chippewas who had for months been awaiting the delivery of promised annuities in the form of pork, flour, beans, and bacon. But when the *Palmyra* came to rest at the future site of Stillwater, a crew of thirty-six millhands proceeded to unload the machinery for the first sawmill on the St. Croix. The disappointed Indians began to shower the steamboat with boulders, and the *Palmyra's* captain, remembering his newly installed steam whistle, let go with a blast that scattered the Chippewas for miles into the woods.

So the sawmill was erected on the riverbank. That

winter the thud of axes sounded through the valley and in the spring the logs swarmed down the rushing April current. The whine of the saws became a steady and prophetic voice beside that pine-fringed river.

Simple as these operations were, the volume of lumber grew steadily down the Mississippi. Every river led to rich tracts of pine and the stream itself was the road to market. By 1850 developments were growing in all the great Wisconsin pineries and sawmill towns were springing up on the six great lumber rivers—the Wisconsin, Black, Red Cedar, St. Croix, Chippewa, and Wolf.

In the sawmills changes came quickly to meet the growing trade in finished lumber. The rotary saw replaced the crude "muley" saw and cut twenty times as much lumber in a day's shift. Promptly millmen learned how ruthless that whirling blade could be, and in time the familiar warning passed into common speech: "Don't monkey with the buzz saw."

With the rotary saw spitting its spray of sawdust and the multiple blades snarling through great logs, a mill crew was never far fram danger. Every mill town had its men with mutilated hands. Over and over they told the story of big Olaf's explaining to the foreman how he had just lost a finger. The foreman thought the saws were guarded, but Olaf demonstrated how it had happened: "Vell, Ae tak da boord dis vay wit' dis hand an' dis vay wit' da oder. Ae move da boord op to da machine lak dat, an da first ting Ae know—YUMPIN YIMINY, DAR GOES ANODER VON!"

While the early camps crept up the rivers the forest appeared inexhaustible. Like sod huts on the Dakota plain, the lumber shanties were lost in immensity. The mutter of the ax seemed a feeble threat to that unmapped country with its never-trodden swamps and impenetrable hillsides. But men who would soon be millionaires had seen the rich timber that centuries had produced. And other men had dreamed of townsites on the prairies and cities at the junctions of rivers. After the Civil War there was a forty-year frenzy in the pine woods; to build the West, the northern forests were laid waste. Logging had become a big business.

CHAPTER 18

Men Against the Forest

A GOOD cruiser, the old saying ran, was born to the trade.

Swan Helstrom was a good one. In fact he was famous. He cruised timber through the wildest and roughest country of the North, from the Tomahawk River all the way up Keweenaw Peninsula in Lake Superior.

Picture him with his blond hair and his blue eyes, six-feet-three on his snowshoes or in his moccasins, traveling over rough country with a hundred pounds of supplies and equipment on his back. He is fifty miles from the nearest settlement and he'll be many miles farther before he swings around south again. Instinctively he finds his way through country no white man has ever seen before, and all the time his mind is busy: locating his range by a pocket compass, counting his paces, sweeping the forest with his keen blue eyes, sorting out pine from the rest of the timber, studying the soil to judge what lies out of sight (white pine in heavy soil, jack pine and Norway pine in lighter soil), his memory recording this country like a camera. At the end of the day, while his kettle boils on the fire, he jots down his notes: the terrain he has been over, what running water he has found, the various stands of timber in that section, and to the thousand board feet what the pine tracts will produce. A day's work. And there will be many days passing through swamp and along pine-shadowed rivers before he changes his campfire for a supper table. Alert, resourceful, intuitive, he knows the forest like a Chippewa and he carries whole counties in his mind. Whole counties without a footprint in them, except his own.

This man with the slow smile and the gentle sing-song voice, like wind and like water, had the most skilled trade in all the North.

As logging grew into its epic proportions, every company sent cruisers into new country to bring back reports of potential lumber production. Behind the cruiser came the big camps, the tote roads, the spring rivers choked with a billion feet of pine, the whine and snarl of the mills. He was a forerunner of the whole vast enterprise.

Yet the cruiser was a man of the forest who lived off the country for whole seasons at a stretch. Between cruising assignments he turned back instinctively to the woods. A natural hunter, he might turn professional for a season, sledding great loads of deer, elk, bear, wolves, wildcats to the railroad to be shipped to the Chicago game markets. Einer Brandt, a veteran Norwegian cruiser in Pierce County along the Mississippi, once killed ninety-six deer and three elk between Thanksgiving and Christmas. One day in the following spring he shot a bear and three cubs and caught the fourth cub alive. He carried all five of them seven miles back to town, the live one inside his shirt. When he got there he said the live one gave him more trouble than all the others put together.

Timber cruising attracted hardy men who were not afraid of the loneliness of remote country. There were noted Irish and French-Canadian cruisers, and there were occasional halfbreeds who chose to follow this lonely and demanding life. But inevitably many of the cruisers were Norse woodsmen. In the mind of this race was a kinship with the wilderness. They were men of powerful frame, and they were woodsmen at heart. They were at home in a tamarack swamp or under the moan of pine boughs. For they were an elemental people, hardy and resourceful, meditative and self-contained. They marked the way up hidden rivers, into the gloom of ancient forests.

So, on the site of Swan Helstrom's remote camp-fires grew the big camps. The great lumber companies drove their logging roads into the rich pinelands and set up the buildings in a trampled clearing: a bunk-house, a cookhouse, an office, stables, hay sheds, and granaries. In the boom years of the seventies and eighties a camp might house a hundred men who would cut many millions of feet of pine in the five-month frozen season.

Gone was the great silence of the winter woods.

CHAPTER 19

Boomtime on the Skid Road

In late October, when the air grew crisp and a web of ice spread over the rivers before daylight, the lumberjacks began to gather in the northern towns. They came in from a summer's work on the Great Lakes or in the harvest fields, and for a few weeks they thronged the streets of Florence, Rhinelander, Wausau, Chippewa Falls, Eau Claire, Stillwater, Duluth, Brainerd, Cloquet.

Before their summer's wage was squandered in the saloons that lined the sawdust streets, they counted out greenbacks in the supply stores and piled their outfit on the counter: high leather boots, woolen pants and socks, gumshoes, heavy woolen shirts, plaid mackinaws. With the donning of their winter garb, the spirit of the woods came back to them. They strolled the streets together, their calked boots ringing on the sidewalks, their jaunty woolen caps pushed back on their heads. Their sky-blue mackinaws and scarlet pants filled the town with color.

While the loggers strolled the streets, stopping in at the Mammoth Bar or the Peerless Saloon, the lumbermen were sitting around the big heater, stoked with four-foot cordwood, in the Northern House, planning the season's operations. Already their foremen were in the woods with a gang of swampers, setting up the camps, laying out the tote roads, and surveying the timber to be cut.

Rumors went quickly through the streets and grew in the hotels and boardinghouses: International was out to hire a thousand men, Northwest was outfitting seven camps up Swan River, Weyerhaeuser was going to log the Little Flambeau. In the woods the big steam overhead skidders were being rigged, and the tote roads needed only freezing to be ready for the sleds.

When the agents pushed their way into the saloons and began to sign up crews, the men crowded around them, eager to begin the hard life and the grueling work, thirteen hours a day at twenty below zero. A few months before, many of them had declared they'd never go back to the woods, they'd starve first. But when the first snows came they remembered the long tables loaded with smoking platters of pork and tubs of rice pudding, the axes ringing in the air, the raised cry *Tim-mber-r-r! Down the line!* and the friendly reek of the crowded bunkhouse, the tales and songs from the deacon seat, and they were ready for the camps again.

From a hundred different lives they came, and it was a varied crew that shouldered their heavy "turkeys," the logger's bag, and climbed aboard the trains. In the boom years the Scandinavians came to the woods in great numbers, till every camp held scores of Norwegians, Swedes, and Finns. They towered above the wiry little Scotsmen and the catlike French Canadians. Half a dozen languages sounded in the streets of lumber towns when the jacks were gathering, and in the camps the woods slang was the only common speech.

At camp the men became a unit, working, eating,

smoking, sleeping together, a hundred of them organized to mow a swath through the forest. Once in the woods, fifty miles from any settlement, their beards grew black and their hands hardened quickly at the familiar toil. For a dollar a day they would turn out two hours before daybreak and work like demons till after dark.

By the first gray daylight the men were at their places in the woods. The seesaw clang of the crosscut was a prelude to the long cry *Tim-mber-r-r! Down the line! Watch out!* The swampers, the "punk hunters," and a second team of sawyers took their turns at it, and the huge pine was reduced to saw logs ready for the heavy branding ax that identified them with the company mark—a pollywog Y for the Shaw Company, a double X for Weyerhaeusers, a gable and a cross for the Hamilton logs, and other marks as various as cattle brands on the western plains. Then horses dragged the logs over the swampers' trail to the skidway where they were loaded in a huge pyramid on the log sled and clamped together with chains. Mounted on the crest of his pyramid of pine, the driver's voice rang in the cold air. *Hyah! Huddup! Huddup in there!* and thirty thousand feet of logs moved toward the river landing.

Such prodigious loads were possible only because of the ice roads that had been introduced in the Mississippi pineries by Michigan lumbermen. Every night the road monkeys drove their tank sprinklers to insure a fresh coating of ice in the grooves worn by the sled runners. As an assistant each teamster had his "hayman on the hill" who sprinkled hay or sand on steep places to check the momentum of the load. But despite all precautions the teamster had a daredevil's job. Many a "bull cook" in the camps hobbled about the cookhouse on crippled legs; that was the only lumber job left for a teamster whose load had fallen on him.

At noon, standing in a box sled among steaming kettles of beans, beef stew, and tea, the bull cook drove over the tote road to a central point in the woods. When he blew his dinner horn that carried five miles through the snowy forest, and raised his wolflike howl, *Ye-ow! 'S goin' to waste!* the men swarmed in from every direction. Though they ate around a big fire of slash, the beans froze on their plates and the tea froze in their whiskers.

At night they came into camp stamping with cold and grim with hunger. In the cookhouse the long tables were loaded with food: smoking platters of fresh meat, bowls of mashed potatoes, piles of pancakes and pitchers of corn syrup, kettles of rich brown beans, pans of prunes, dried peaches, rice puddings, rows of apple pies. The monotonous bread and beans of the lumber shanty was only a memory; the big camps fed the men bountifully and well. (At the peak of its activity, the Alger-Smith Company's grocery bill to one Duluth wholesale firm was $250,000 annually.)

The jacks ate silently, with great speed. If a greenhorn was tempted to make conversation at his meals, he was reminded by a placard on the wall: "No talking at the tables." The cooks wanted the men to eat and get out; the men wanted no distraction while food was before them. When the meal was over, they crossed the trampled frozen campyard to the bunkhouse. They pulled off their boots, lit their pipes for an hour's smoke, and then turned in. They slept in double-deck bunks with ends toward the center of the room. The jacks called them "muzzle-loaders."

The cook was the "king bee" of camp. He was well-paid and worth his pay, handling prodigious quantities of food, baking, roasting, frying, stewing for a hundred men who ate like horses, feeding them lavishly on an allowance of thirty cents a day per man.

From the earliest days a lumber cook was known by his beans, and this is the way he performed his miracle: he soaked the beans all day, and when supper was over he scalded them and set them steaming by the fire. Then he sliced an onion into the pot, the sweet tang of it rising in the air. Slowly he stirred molasses into the steaming beans and, as a final garnishing, he crisscrossed the pot with strips of fat white pork. Then he sealed the pot and buried it among the embers in the bean hole. By breakfast time they were a rich and golden dish that haunted a lumberjack's memory.

Assisting the cook was the bull cook—"cookee," he was called in the Wisconsin camps. Though he was the butt of many camp jokes, no one was better liked than the hobbling old fellow who tended the fires in the iron stoves, fetched the wood and the water, peeled the potatoes, and scoured the pans. It was he who rousted the men out in the morning, filling the bunkhouse with the din of his five-foot horn or ringing his cowbell up and down the bunkrows. *Roll out! Tumble out! Daylight in the swamp!* Before he had finished his cry there was a rain of hobnailed boots around him. But his next call was welcome—*Come and get it! Breakfast on the boards!* The men scalded themselves awake with coffee, crammed their stomachs full of pancakes, hash, and beans, and had a bit of banter for the bull cook while they pulled on their mackinaws and rubbed the stiffness out of their mittens.

Apart from the woods crew were the road monkeys, the teamsters, and the stable boss. The teamsters had their own skill, which in a miraculous way they imparted to their horses; a woods team could handle enormous loads on those icy ways with almost uncanny intelligence. The teamsters had a longer day than the cutting crew. At four in the morning, hours before daylight, they were in the stable, feeding, cleaning, and harnessing their teams. Then they returned to the bunkhouse, washed their hands in the big barrel that stood inside the door, and took a chew of plug tobacco as an appetizer for breakfast.

A famous teamster in the Hamilton camps was Ed Erickson. Like all Scandinavian woodsmen, he loved his tobacco, and somehow his horses had acquired that fondness. Whenever he pulled the plug from his pocket his horses turned their heads expectantly, and he had to give them each a chew before he put the plug away. One winter he ran up such a bill at the wannagan that he didn't have much of a payday left. "Dose damn horses," he said bitterly, "keep me broke buyin' 'em chewin' t'bacco."

One stormy April night at the beginning of the drive he made a hurried trip to town with a drowned corpse, six men who had run picks and peaveys into their feet, and six hundred pounds of dynamite. When he reached the station Ed drew a long breath and grumbled: "By da sawed-off, blue-eyed, holy old

mackinaw, da vorst be-devil damn load Ae ever hauled
—von dead man, six cripples, an' six boxes o' dynamite. An' Ae could of lit my pipe wit' da lightnin'
any minute."

The lure of the camps brought unexpected men
to join the gang of unskilled swampers who cleared
brush and lopped off branches from the fallen trees.
It was not uncommon to find a soft-spoken man, with
thoughtful eyes and the long thin fingers that never
belonged to a woodsman, reading a leather-bound
book in the lamplight and talking about New York
and Boston as another man would talk about Stillwater and Reads Landing. One winter in the Luding-
ton camps there were two English ministerial gradu-
ates—one was reported to be a victim of whisky, the
other of marriage. It was said they got away by themselves on Sunday and talked all day in an undertone.

All kinds of toil went into logging, the endurance
of the sawyers, the ponderous strength of the skidders,
the craft of the choppers, the quick skill of the
loaders, the instinct of the teamsters. And all kinds of
men made up the camp. It was a cosmos ringed by
the immense desolation of the winter woods, raising
its din against primeval silence. That small world contained old men and young men, shrewd men who
would themselves be known among the lumber barons
before the pineries were gone, and slow-witted swampers whose hands would always be horned with toil,
clear-eyed youths from the northern settlements and
men whose faces shielded memory.

But with all their variety, logging put a common

stamp upon them. In the woods they wore the common uniform of wool cap and mackinaw, and after a few weeks the life of the wilderness gave them a common character. They became rollicking and primitive men, possessed with enormous energy, enormous appetites, enormous endurance, a fiery zest burning in them all winter long.

CHAPTER 20

Skylarking Jack

NINE o'clock was the usual bedtime in camp, but on Saturday night there would be a genuine "hurrah," games and songs and dancing till midnight. The evening began with cards, played with tobacco for stakes. After an hour of this quiet diversion, the bunkhouse was thick with smoke and the men were growing restless. Somebody called for the fiddle, and the noise began.

A fiddle was as essential in camp as a tote road. Sometimes there was also a mouth organ or an accordion. The lumberjack fiddler had his own style of playing, timed like a crosscut saw in a log. He set the fiddle flat against his chest, thumped loudly with his right foot, and used only the middle six inches of the bow. He might begin with "The Festive Lumberjack" or "The Pokegama Bear" and then swing into "The Big Eau Claire" with a mother's warning to her daughter about marrying a lumberjack.

And stealing logs and shingle bolts, and telling awful lies,
And playing cards and swearing is all their exercise.
So if you want to marry for comfort or for joy
I advise you to get married to an honest farmer's boy.

Soon someone would call for "The Little Brown Bulls," and the fiddle sharpened quickly while the men took hold of the words:

Not a thing on the river McCluskey did fear
When he drew the stick o'er the big spotted steers.
They were young, quick and sound, girting eight foot three,
Said McCluskey to the foreman, "They're the ladies for me!"

A clear tenor voice was in great demand in the
bunkhouse. Many a foreman took pains to see that he
got a good lead singer when he was making up his
crew; good spirit in the bunkhouse meant bigger cuttings in the woods. The day after Christmas, 1877, a
Scotsman came into Camp 5 on Fever River looking
for work. When the foreman asked if he could sing
he immediately began "Bonnie Doon" in a fine tenor
voice. After that, as Bill Alft put it, "he couldn't get
away."

Some of the camp ballads were bawdy and boisterous, but many also were melancholy with the sentiment of wandering men. These were crude verses,
mirroring a life harder and more hazardous than most.
And they were sung to simple, plaintive airs, letting
loneliness show through. A man can sing what he can
never say.

> A lumberjack's life is a wearisome one
> Although some say it's free from care.
> It's the swinging an ax from morning to night
> In the forests wild and drear.
>
> Or sleeping in the bunkhouse dreary
> While the winter winds do blow;
> But as soon as the morning star does appear
> To the wild woods must we go.

A lumberjack's life was not all beans and pan-cakes, and hot coffee to wash them down. It was also hardship, toil, and danger, and a knowledge of death.

> The rapids they were raging,
> The waters were so high.
> Says the foreman to Swan Swanson
> "This jam we'll have to try."
>
> Swan Swanson answered like a man,
> "That's what I aim to do."
> But while he spoke the jam it broke
> And Swanson he went through.

By this time the men were restless again and ready for a rousing game of Hot Bottom, Shuffle the Brogan, or Buy My Sheep. These were noisy and spirited games, essentially alike in that the monot-onous point of them all was the inflicting of blows, usually with an oversized gumshoe, upon some un-suspecting lumberjack's rear. But that was point enough for these fellows. They laughed till the room shook when a good resounding whack was landed.

A Saturday night hurrah could not be concluded without a dance. Men with bandannas tied around their arms played the part of women, and in their bare feet the jacks jigged through the haze of smoke. Sometimes a man had to stop to take the splinters out of his feet, for the pine floor was pitted and rough with the print of hobnails. They danced to a variety of tunes jerked out on the screeching fiddle: "Devil's Dream," "Money Musk," "Old Dan Tucker," "Pop Goes the Weasel!" After a final noisy dance they sprawled on the deacon

seat, knocked out their pipes, and a few silent men who had been sitting there all along threw away the miniature pike poles and cant hooks they had been whittling. They all yawned and crawled into the bunks, with the delicious knowledge that they could sleep late Sunday morning.

Sunday was boil-up day in camp. A big lard can was placed over an open fire outdoors and there each lumberjack in turn boiled and scrubbed his clothes. Occasionally a man got out his razor for a shave, but most of the jacks were satisfied to comb their beards and cut each other's hair. The cook served a special dinner on Sunday, often a roast meat and a cobbler pudding. After dinner the men patched clothes, sewed on buttons, and played games of checkers and cards.

If the quiet palled, there were always the greenhorns to haze. Favorite practical jokes were to send a greenhorn to the cook shanty to borrow the bean hole or to the camp office for a "crosshaul" or a "round turn." When the irate cook or the foreman drove the greenhorn out, the jacks nearly split their sides with laughing. These jokes, of course, were based on lumberjack slang, with such terms as these:

crosshaul: a track at right angles to a logging road
round turn: the circular track where teamsters turned around
gazabo: any worker
deacon seat: benches beneath the bunkrows in the bunkhouse
pike: supply road leading into camp
push or big push: camp foreman
sky-hooking: stacking logs on top of load
ground hog: man who directed logs with his peavy as they were rolled up to load

blue: a log that rolled out of line because larger at one end
than the other
to Saginaw a log: to retard the large end
to St. Croix a log: to help the small end gain
gumming a log: failing to keep the two ends even
getting a stem cracked: breaking a leg
flaggins: dinner in the woods
wannagan: camp commissary, from which the men bought
everything from mackinaws to "the makin's"
logging berries: prunes
cold shuts (emergency links for mending chain): fried-
cakes
long greens or hay: bills in pay envelope
turkey: the duffle bag containing a jack's belongings
sky pieces: hats
nose bags: haversacks for carrying a cold lunch

Until he learned the logging vernacular a newcomer was more than a greenhorn; he was likely to be
in the way, and he might easily get a leg mashed beneath a log or caught in a set of tackle. Once he knew
the language, he was not so easy a victim for practical
jokes and he could jump clear before a saw log hurtled
through the brush. He was on his way to becoming a
genuine lumberjack.

CHAPTER 21

Immortals In Mackinaws—Paul Bunyan's Crew

A HURRAH came only once a week, but every evening in the bunkhouse there was an hour for smoking and yarning. The men all smoked Peerless cut plug tobacco, called "Scandihoovian" in the camps. This was a strong black product—a combination, according to Bill Alft, of "jimson weed, old rope, and burdock." Bill said it got its name because "when it was smoked in Wisconsin, people could smell it in Scandihoovia."

When the barrel stove glowed cherry red, sending up a cloud of steam from the frozen socks, mittens, and mackinaws on the drying racks, the room quickly filled with such a fog that a man could not see the door fifteen feet away. In that rich and friendly stench the jacks luxuriated. They stretched out on the deacon seat, yawning with the relish of men who had worked all day in the cold air and have their bellies crammed with supper. From their pipes they blew out a thickening haze of smoke till the kerosene lamps were haloed and the pictures from the *Police Gazette* were indistinguishable on the wall. There was nothing to read, and these were not reading men. They yawned and yarned, their big voices booming with lazy banter and finally giving way to the melancholy twanging of a Jew's harp somewhere on the deacon seat.

This is the setting for one of the few series of immortal literature that America has produced. For now the jacks are in the mood for storytelling.

You can tell a lot about people from their slang and from their stories. In all the beautiful and varied speech of men there has never been a richer, racier slang than the "logger's lingo" that developed in the Mississippi pineries. Never was there a lore so exuberant and heroic, so comic and so epic as the lumberjack tales that grew up in the smoke-filled bunkhouse. This is the wildest, freshest folklore in the world, profoundly American with its love of wilderness and physical exploit and yet colored by the imagination of all the races of men who worked in the great woods.

Lounging on the deacon seat were the wilderness Homers, creating magnificent myths.

The stories which the men told through that haze of smoke were about their own life and their own calling, but lifted into boasting, dread, and glory. There were epic tales of battles, for these men were fighters, battles against blizzards, floods, and log jams. There were tales of record cuttings and of immortal rivalries between camps. There were sagas of warfare between crews across the river—scarlet bloodstains on the snow.

These were actual enough. But Jack had a fantastic imagination as well as a vivid memory. So there were ghost stories of the gloomy woods, stories of cruisers who went into new country and never came out again, whose trails were followed till they ended all at once in mystery and nothing. There were legends of great beasts that prowled along the tote road. The most fearsome of these was the evil, mysterious "agropelter," infuriated by the loggers' invasion of his precinct. This creature lived in hollow trees and dropped great limbs on passers-by. Only one man had come away from an encounter with the monster—big Ole Kittelson, cruising on the St. Croix, who had such a hard head that the limb broke into bits and Big Ole dropped his turkey and ran twelve miles in his fright.

Living long in the deep woods did not bring contempt for its mysteries. In the woodsman's mind the eerie twilight was haunted by grotesque creatures. Sometimes it was a distorted fear that sounded in the stories, and often it was the logger's grotesque humor laughing through his superstition.

So came into being the many strange forest creatures that lived only in their tales. There was the gilly grouse that nested near the Big Onion River and laid square eggs which Paul Bunyan's men used for dice. Every logger knew of the mysterious ax-handle hound that prowled all night about the camps devouring ax and peavey handles, so that it was no wonder a man lost everything he didn't put under cover. There was that enigma, the tote-road shagamaw, with the claws of a bear on its front legs and the hoofs of a moose behind. This monster prowled along the tote roads devouring coats and mittens which it found on stumps and logs. It was a shy and harmless beast, but still a man hates to lose his mackinaw. And strangest of all was the great hoop snake that rolled through the woods all winter with its tail in its mouth. Once this snake stung a peavey handle, causing it to swell so that Paul Bunyan cut a thousand cords of stovewood from it.

About these tales there was a whole mythology of

men like gods who logged in fabulous countries.
Sprawled on the deacon seat the jacks never tired of
repeating their exploits. The great foreman, Olaf Olaf-
son, beat the Irish crew into the water with his cut and
then drove his logs all the day down to the Gulf of
Mexico because they needed bridge timbers down there.
Another hero, Jigger Jones, could walk a felled spruce
barefoot and kick off every knot from but to tip. The
powerful Jean Frechette once stepped up to a three-
hundred-pound cask of log chain, took a good hold of
it and loaded it onto a sleigh. This was a great feat,
but Big Ole, looking on, muttered something derisive.
Then he walked over to a horse that stood near by and
lifted it up till its four legs were kicking in the air.

All these figures were familiar to the men on the
deacon seat. They had invented them out of their own
lives. So they told about Gus Gunderson, the camp foreman on Tadpole River, who invented the logger's lingo;
of Chris Crosshaulson who succeeded Gus after he had
lost his voice and so lost his authority; of the greatest
foreman of them all, Hels Helson the mighty Swede,
the Bull of the Woods, who logged off all the Smiling
River country in one winter.

These last were some of Paul Bunyan's men, and
there was a whole gallery of others: Johnny Inkslinger
whom Paul found beside Twin Rivers, a little man but
educated, with a necktie on and many pencils behind
his ears, so Paul made him his timekeeper; and Big Ole,
the blacksmith, who had to be careful not to sink his
hammer through his anvil; and Happy Olsen; and Old
Time Sandy; and of course Babe, the great blue ox,

who had to be watered always below a dam for fear he'd drink the millpond dry.

And there was Paul himself in his snug blue cap and his plaid mackinaw. Paul Bunyan was a great lumberjack, but he was more than that. A simple job of logging was not enough for him. He had the discontent of greatness; he was pestered by imagination; he wanted to make history. Ever since that first Winter of the Blue Snow, when he lived in the vast cave with his books and his traps and his blankets, using a trimmed pine tree for a pencil, he had been a dreamer. He dreamed of great drives and great cuttings, and no matter what great things he did he was still a dreamer, always figuring on next season and the biggest feats of all.

The French Canadians had started the stories. They were quick-witted, imaginative, and superstitious; for a hundred years, from Maine to Minnesota, they kept the legends going. Paul was a Canuck himself—Paul Bonhomme of the Two Mountain country the early stories told about. The stories first took shape in the New Brunswick camps, where the men began to talk of a great camp foreman who could lift a snagged pine log over a blowdown and could carry five hundred pounds on a portage. And there probably, or later in Maine, the English tongue turned Bonhomme into Bunyan. A camp boss was the law in his camp; he had to possess courage and strength to dominate his men. Such a boss was Paul Bunyan, and the folk imagination flowered about him.

The tales of this mighty logger spread south to Maine and west to Quebec and Michigan. The Americans in the camps improved on the stories, at first in burlesque of the originals. But Paul Bunyan was too genuine a hero, too magnificent a myth to succumb to parody; he won the scoffers to discipleship, and soon the Americans were creating legends of their own. As the stories traveled, Paul Bunyan took his place among the local heroes, Jigger Jones, Jean Frechette, and Joe Mufraw who drove calks into his boots in the shape of his initials and could kick his mark in a ceiling eight feet high. But Paul was stronger than the other gods. He was more picturesque and lasting; he was immortal.

Though Paul himself was a Canuck, the loggers in the American pineries gave him his true properties. They gave him Babe, the great blue ox that measured forty-two ax handles and a plug of chewing tobacco between the eyes. They created for him the fabulous logging camp with its enormous cookhouse and the pile of prune stones darkening the window and the ax-handle hounds slinking over the campyard sniffing for peaveys. They provided the chipmunks that feasted on the prune stones and grew so ferocious that Paul's men shot them for tigers, and the mosquitoes that straddled the rivers picking off lumberjacks from the log drive. They added to Paul the minor heroes of his camps—Big Ole, the blacksmith, and Happy Olsen, and Johnny Inkslinger, and all the rest. They devised the chronology that charted his rule of the woods from the Winter of the Blue Snow to the Spring the Rain Came Up from China. By 1870 he was a full-fledged deity, and in the next fifty years his fame completed its spread across the continent. Paul Bunyan became the logger's god from Maine to Oregon.

Sitting in the fog of the deacon seat, the Scandinavians listened with their big ears, contentment and naïve wonder on their earnest faces. They were men about whom myths could gather—mighty of bone and sinew, taciturn, the original "big silent men of the spaces," hardy and resourceful when their hands had a job to manage, courageous and enduring. Nothing was too difficult for them. They were at home in the woods as other men were at home in towns. So they heard their own kind immortalized in American folk-lore: Big Ole and Axel Axelson and Chris Crosshaulson taking their place among Paul Bunyan's men, performing great feats on the Pyramid Forty and beside the rivers of legend.

CHAPTER 22

Pike-Pole and Peavey

WHEN spring came in the woods and the tote road softened, cutting operations were at an end. Now the crew were lumberjacks no longer, but rivermen. They exchanged ax and saw for pike pole, cant hook, and peavey; and they changed their low rubbers for calked boots that would bite into the pine logs. Their woolen pants were replaced by overalls, as a lighter garb for men who would often be waist-deep in swirling water. Rivermen always wore their overalls "stagged," cut off just above the boot tops. The stagging was done with an ax, the aim being to make the edges as ragged as possible. Usually one leg was cut shorter than the other.

The driving crews were the pick of the camps, men of great strength, hardihood, and daring. They had to risk accident and death a dozen times a day. They had to wade icy water and dodge the battering rams of saw logs in the rapids. They had to go hungry for days at a time, to work without sleep or even rest, and to go soaked to the skin when snowbanks were still white along the rivers.

As soon as the ice was out of the river, when the water was at its crest, the rivermen, armed with mauls and handspikes, crouched under the great pile of logs on the landing and began "breaking" the rollways. With a mutter and a roar the whole winter's cut of timber plunged into the stream. The swift water boiled upward. Down the ice-cold torrent a hundred thousand logs surged and hurtled. The drive was on.

Now for a few weeks the driving streams were crammed, crowded, and studded with great pine trunks bound for the sawmills or the rafting booms; the whole vast current of them grinding and twisting over the shallows and around the bends. Sometimes the lead logs halted at an obstruction and piled up in ragged masses. Then the enormous pressure drove them forward with a sound like thunder. Above the roar of logs and the submerged rushing of water rose the shouts of the rivermen riding that flood of timber.

With long iron-tipped pike poles the driving crew guided the headlong tide. Across waterfalls, around bends, through sluiceways, and the spray of rapids, the logs must be kept moving toward the mills. Leaping tirelessly over that mass of timber, the "white water birlers" rode in the vanguard. One of their favorite feats was to ride a log through the sluiceway, where it was hurtled downward at an angle of thirty to forty-five degrees. The second crew followed the rear of the drive, picking up logs that were stranded, herding the sluggish and waterlogged timbers into the living current.

At driving season the wannagan was no longer the camp office in the woods but the floating shack, built on a raft, which came downstream in the rear of the drive. It housed the cook, his supplies and utensils, a first-aid kit for men who sprained their ankles or ran pike poles into their feet, and some extra pike poles and peaveys for men who had their tools broken or

wrenched out of their hands and lost. When the drive was moving smoothly, the men waited in shifts till the wannagan came swirling along and ate fairly regular meals from the cook's larder. Often this was not possible, and the crew had to snatch a bite from the nose bags which they carried strapped on their shoulders. Frequently all thought of food was crowded out of their minds by the necessity to guard against a slowing up of the great tide of timber.

Sometimes, in spite of all vigilance and precautions, a solid jam piled up. Soon acres of timber were frozen in chaos and the whole long drive was hung up halfway down to the mill. Over this confused and treacherous mass the drivers ranged in their ironshod boots, seeking the key logs that held the jam together. With a skillful thrusting of the pike pole, a driver could set the whole log-locked river free. But when the jam was broken the pent timbers churned and hurtled with release. Many a daring fellow was lost in that wild rush of struggling pine. Rivermen's bodies were seldom found.

One great jam filled the Mississippi above Brainerd for sixteen days. The crew worked themselves to exhaustion, but the tangle was too deep and intricate to move. The foreman sent down the river for dynamite and the rivermen went to town. They gathered in the saloons on Front Street: Number One, Last Turn, and the famous Dolly Varden Club. After a run of pay cards at mustang and chuck-a-luck, Otto Olsen decided to quit the drive. He entered the hundred-mile roller skating contest in the amusement palace and, paired off with Abba Hall, he won the prize by covering the distance in seven and a half hours. By that time he felt so prosperous that he went to the Headquarters House, Brainerd's famous hotel which boasted "over six hundred joints of stovepipe." But he couldn't sleep there because a minister kept walking up and down the corridors rehearsing his sermon. So Otto went back to the wannagan and rejoined the drive. The dynamite arrived and the rivermen packed it among the tangled timbers. At last the long call was relayed up the winding river of logs— *Greenhorns ashore!* Five blasts echoed over the forest and the lead logs began to haul. With a grinding plunge and thunder the jam gave way.

That night Otto Olsen danced on a surging river of pine.

CHAPTER 23

"Dandy, Handy Raftsman Jim"

MANY of the woodsmen lived the year round with logs. All winter they were lumberjacks. In the spring they were rivermen, riding the great drive down to the booming yards. All summer they were raftsmen, taking the enormous Mississippi rafts down the river to Burlington, Quincy, and St. Louis.

The great assembly point for logs was at Beef Slough, near the mouth of the Chippewa River. Beef Slough was named before the era of lumber; in the 1820's a government boat loaded with beef cattle for the garrison at Fort Snelling grounded on a sand bar where the Chippewa enters the Mississippi. To lighten the boat's draft the cattle were goaded into the water, where they splashed and waded ashore. The boat then passed over the bar and the cattle were reloaded at a shelving bank a little distance upstream. From that day the shallows became known as Beef Slough.

With the lumber era Beef Slough became famous. Taking advantage of the quiet water in the shoals, the Beef Slough Logging Company put in an extensive system of sheer booms to enclose logs floated down the Chippewa. When the booming yards were full there were twenty miles of logs backed up and waiting. Across the mouth of the boom, logs were led out and formed into rafts for the run down to the mills.

Small rafts, along with the spring drive of head-long timber, came down the tributary rivers, but it was in the big booming yards of Beef Slough and Reads Landing that the "Mississippi raft" took shape. Three brails of logs made a unit 700 feet long and 135 feet wide, which rivermen called "half a raft." In seasons of low water half a raft was all that could safely be taken downriver. But when the river was full rafts were made of six brails, bound together with checkworks, crosslines, "A" lines, and corner lines. These Mississippi rafts approached the incredible size of 1,500 by 300 feet.

In the center of this island of pine was the cook-shed, where the cook slept and prepared meals for the crew of twenty to thirty-five men. The crew slept in a shed at the stern of the raft and the pilot in a lonely cell of his own at the forward end where he had a free view of the river channel. Planks were laid along the ends of the raft to provide footing for the men who worked the sweeps. Lengthwise down the center ran a plank for the pilot, who paced up and down, eying the channel, study-ing the wind and the current and watching the raft's movement with wary eyes. When the vast hulk was to swing, he called out: "Left behind, right in front!" or "Right behind, left in front!" and the men leaped to their places and leaned in unison against the long sweeps.

Raft pilots became famous men on the river. They were skilled, courageous, uncanny in their memory and miraculous in the instinct that told them of shifting bars and treacherous currents. From the first years of lumbering operations on the Black, Chippewa, and St.

Croix rivers, in the 1830's, pilots were required to run the timber rafts down the Mississippi. The pioneer steamboat pilots learned their trade in that hard school —men like Louis de Marah, Louis Moreau and Pleasant Carmack. Perhaps the most picturesque of the raft pilots was Joe Guardapie, a French-Chippewa half-breed. He was a lithe and stealthy-footed man who could whip any burly roustabout who ever questioned his commands; it was said that in case of necessity he could put a dozen of them to rout. He spoke a rich mixture of broken English, French and Chippewa, all seasoned with Anglo-Saxon profanity; and if that language failed he had another, made up of a hard fist and a heavy boot.

There were other storied men. Sandy McPhail with his famous red beard and Charlie La Pointe with his shrewd blue eyes left memories of their mastery of river currents and of men. But by the old accounts the most skillful of all the raft pilots was Stephen Hanks, a cousin of Abe Lincoln, who piloted great rafts through the forty years when lumber was the overwhelming commerce on the Upper Mississippi. He knew every bend and sand bar, every towhead and crosscurrent from Stillwater to St. Louis.

Until after the Civil War log rafts were floated down the Mississippi with no power but the river current. In local reaches of slack water towboats came into their first use on the upper river, but the river current was still the prime mover of the lumber commerce. From the famous logging town of Stillwater, on the St. Croix River, log rafts were often pushed by towboats to Prescott, at the juncture of the St. Croix and the Mississippi.

From Prescott the rafts drifted to Lake Pepin, and when the current failed in Lake Pepin they were propelled again by towboats to Reads Landing at the foot of the lake. From there the clumsy, slow-moving rafts drifted to their destination at Winona, La Crosse, Clinton, Le Claire, Hannibal or St. Louis. If the raft were bound to an Iowa, Illinois, or Missouri port preparations for the long journey were made at Prescott. Stores of pork, beans, flour, molasses, whisky were piled in the cookshed, and the braces and crosslines of the raft were carefully overhauled. While these preparations were in progress the rafting crews bantered with each other on the riverside and often they came to blows as they strode the streets of Prescott at the end of the day's work. Rival raft crews fought like rival timber crews, sometimes a hundred men tangled together in a single fray. There was little anyone could do until the fight was ended and so people remembered the town marshal sitting on the "snubbing post" with a revolver in his hand, enjoying the scene.

In 1865 steam towing was first tried from Beef Slough to St. Louis. It proved a great saving of time and risk, and soon hundreds of towboats were in use. "Towing," on the Upper Mississippi, meant pushing; the boats were blunt-nosed craft which pushed their load ahead of them. In those years a ballad made up entirely of towboat nomenclature was sung up and down the river: any good riverman knew sixty uninterrupted lines of it.

The *Fred Weyerhaeuser* and the *Frontenac*,
The *F. C. A. Denckman* and the *Sandy Mac*,
The *Menominee* and the *Louisville*,

The *R. J. Wheeler* and the *Jessie Bill*,
The *Robert Semple* and the *Golden Gate*,
The *J. C. Caffery* and the *Sucker State*.

Piloting log rafts remained a hard and skilled job, even though a towboat was there to provide power. The logs drew eighteen inches of water, and it was something of a trick to know where in the shifting, winding, sand-barred, and island-studded Upper Mississippi there were eighteen inches of water for three acres of raft. Further, there remained the hazards of wind and currents and the always precarious business of pushing the great boom of logs around sweeping bends. In rounding curves it was often necessary to loose the crosslines and let the raft bend itself into the shape of the channel. A skilled pilot could bend a raft into a C or even an S in order to get safely through an intricate passage in the river. The famous raft pilots, Joe Guardapie, Stephen Hanks, George Bresseur, Jim McPhail were paid $500 a month, and no one questioned that they earned it. They learned to raft the Mississippi by day and night, when there was not a lighthouse or a channel beacon from St. Anthony's Falls to the Gulf of Mexico. Captain J. M. Turner, a veteran of the rafting trade on the upper river, esti-mated that he had made ten trips annually for fifty years, five hundred miles down and five hundred miles back—a total of half a million miles on the Upper Mis-sissippi. He added, with a complete misunderstanding of arithmetic or geography, that it was equivalent to two trips around the globe.

Despite the greatest boldness and skill of her pilot, a raft could easily come to grief. There were pilots who through bad luck or bad management ran afoul of one obstacle after another in the long journey from the northern booming yards to the mill towns down below. The raft crews had names for pilots who had a habit of misfortune. A pilot who repeatedly hung up a raft on a sand bar was known as a "sticker." If his raft struck bridge piers more than twice in a season he was called a "wood butcher." A pilot with a reputation for ramming steamboats in the stream or scraping them when they lay at landings was a "boat killer."

To keep clear of these ubiquitous hazards a raft pilot needed three gifts—a graphic and tenacious memory, quick and inclusive eyesight, and iron nerves. In addition there was a mysterious faculty, which no one could define but which often meant the difference between safety and disaster, known to the raftsmen as "river sense." If a man didn't possess it his raft was bound for trouble. All the way from Beef Slough to the Blood Island lumberyard at St. Louis there were tight and troublesome places. An old French-Canadian raft pilot named La France had a single term of profanity, "Sacree!" He had abundant use for it. When his raft hit Argo Island he shouted, "Sacree! That island has a good appetite for a raft!" When he was feeling his way through the short bend of a shallow channel it was "Sacree Coon Slough!" But he had the river sense and he took his timber through.

The raft crews were lumberjacks who had quickly squandered their pay from the camp, and their pay from the spring drive, and were now getting five dollars a day for manning a raft from Wabasha to Rock Island or St.

Louis. Still dressed in their stagged trousers, though
they had thrown away their calked boots and went barefoot over the three-acre raft of pine, they slept in their
hut, ate their meals in the sun while the bluffs of Iowa
and Illinois moved by, and were ready night and day to
leap to the great sweeps that would hold their charge
from swinging in a cross-current or blowing into a
slough. A few months ago, with winter locking the
rivers, they had been felling timber in the frozen
swamps. Now they basked in the sun and sang under the
starlight while the Mississippi shores slipped past.

But there was strenuous work for them still, before the raft could be delivered: fighting cross winds
and treacherous currents, sweating at the sweeps
through Maquoketa Slough with no hand left to fight
the smother of mosquitoes, turning out at midnight
to witch a loosening brail together. A raft was at the
mercy of wind because even the towboats had such a
shallow draft that "they could run over a field after
a heavy dew"; and they could not hold a raft that
once began to swing. All craft built for the Upper Mississippi had light draft, none more than five feet, many
much less. The packet *Chippewa Falls*, when light,
drew exactly twelve inches. One day in the low water
of 1864 she grounded on a bar below Hastings, and
after a few minutes floated free. The pilot said he had
shifted his quid of tobacco. They said that when she
struck a bar head on two deck hands stepped out, lifted
her over the bar, and she went on. Because of the peril
of grounding a raft in shallow water, the crew had to
be constantly alert lest they be swept out of the current.
On windy nights they tied up to great oak trunks on

the shore. When the raft moved, the moorings cut deep into the oak and smoked with friction. A man was stationed at each mooring line to douse buckets of water on the tree to keep the rope from bursting into flame.

Raftsmen were known up and down the river as the most rip-roaring of all sons of perdition. When a raft tied up and the crew came to town they began with a dozen rounds of forty-rod whisky and ended with a free-for-all battle in which the barkeeper might be driven out of his saloon and the whole place left a shambles. "A raftsman would just as soon stab you as look at you," said Deacon Condit, who kept the hotel at Le Claire and had been three times to St. Louis. Most people in the river towns were of the opinion that rafting was but a diversion for the crews; their true calling was battle, murder, and sudden death. It was a fact that when a raft tied up at Guttenberg Bend the widow Fowler hid her silver spoons.

Between violent trips ashore the men danced in their bare feet on the logs and wrestled with each other when there was no heavy work to use their energy. For quiet diversions there were hunting and fishing, which could be carried on as they moved down the river. One fine day below the hills of Hannibal, Olsen Skam caught a channel catfish that weighed a hundred and eighty pounds. Jack Grunow made himself a small howitzer and mounted it at the forward end of a raft. He shot into flocks of geese, where they had settled on the sloughs, killing dozens at a shot. He could wade in and gather a good mess of them and still climb aboard the tail end of the raft as it came along.

After a good haul of game or fish the raftsmen sat

down to enjoy a feast. Ahead of them was the excitement of St. Louis, the noisy lighted river-front streets, the lure of women, the floating dance halls that swung in the slow river currents. Overhead were the summer stars. All around them was the murmuring of the great river. So their voices drifted away in the darkness and people in a sleepy river town saw a slow black island moving in the midnight stream. The towboat's riding lights winked in a screen of willow trees, and the wind brought back a tag of song, clear and carefree:

There ain't no cub as cute as him,
Dandy, handy Raftsman Jim.

CHAPTER 24

Towns That Fled Disaster

Bᴀᴄᴋ in the woods above Peshtigo lived a bachelor Swede homesteader, Sven Carlsten. He lived alone on a rise of ground called "Sven's Bluff," but he always kept a woman's petticoat hanging on the wall, because "it make da place seem more homelike."

On rainy days Sven sat in the dim light of his cabin braiding fishlines out of hairs pulled from a horse's tail; he had previously soaked them in water and rolled them pliant on his bare leg, and now he was plaiting the long black threads into a stout strand of fishing line. He lived on fish—fried fish, baked fish, boiled fish: cold fish for his lunch at noon in the woods, smoking-hot fish out of his frying pan for supper. Outside his cabin door he kept a barrel of live fish; it was his larder and it was never empty. But one October morning when he reached in and found but a few small trout darting through his fingers, he knew that his fish were being stolen.

"By gar!" he said to himself, and he worried about it all day in the woods. When he came back it took him five minutes to catch one of the remaining trout for his supper. He frowned heavily over that meal and shook his shaggy head from time to time. "Yust vait," he said darkly when he had put his frying pan away; he had resolved to catch the thief.

That night with a high moon throwing a pale light across his clearing, he sat up in his doorway; but after the moon had set he dropped off to sleep. Sometime later there was a heavy noise at his fish barrel and Sven sprang out of his sleep. In one movement he was beside the barrel, his arms groping for the thief. But he let go quickly when he found himself hugging a big black bear. Wide awake now, Sven lunged back into his cabin, and the bear, crashing like a moose through the thickets, fled into the woods.

"By gar!" Sven said to himself. He had picked up the phrase from the Canucks in the timber and now it seemed to say everything for him.

For three nights the bear did not come back. Meanwhile Sven scrambled down the bluff and caught enough fish to restock the barrel. On the fourth night the bear renewed his thieving. But by that time Sven had an idea.

First, he nearly emptied the barrel of water; then he drove nails into it from all sides so that it was a sharp-studded cylinder above the shallow depth where the fish lay. That night he sat patiently by the door. The moon came up late and in the wan light Sven's big head began to nod. He waked to the sound of claws twanging the stiff barbs of nails and he heard a surprised, impatient grunting. In the faint light he saw the big head rear itself above the open barrel. Then the barrel turned over and the head was swallowed up. With a muffled watery snort the bear and the barrel went into the woods.

"By gar!" said Sven, picking up a trout that glinted on the ground. He never saw bear or barrel again. But in the woods above Peshtigo people still hear a hollow thumping on their stumps at night.

2

About the time Sven Carlsten was waiting to catch his thief, a Norwegian woodsman, Anders Holm, was cruising for Sargent and Bromfield in the rich timber between the Peshtigo and Oconto rivers.

After a month in the woods he ran out of supplies, and on October 8, 1871, he set out for a trading post twelve miles across country. Twelve miles was a short trek for a cruiser who passed over vast tracts of wilderness and scouted out whole counties. Anders expected to be back at his camp before sundown. But he never got back to his camp at all, and he never forgot that eighth day of October. Before he had been an hour on the way he was breathing the mild air thoughtfully, turning his face to the wind and savoring it, while a frown came on his bearded face. When he reached a clearing his eyes confirmed the fear; a smoke haze, already dimming the dark trunks, was thickening in the air.

Fire was not new in the pineries and many a cruiser had learned to pass around a burning stand of timber; but Anders was thinking of the rainless summer, the dry autumn, the acres of slash piled up along the railroad where the swampers had gone through. And his eyes told him what his nostrils had suspected: this fire was not in one direction, but in three. Forgetting now about his own camp and the trading post, he turned south. The wind was rising and it bore a stronger

menace. Now he began to hear the faint and living roar
that is not wind or water, but something more wanton
and dread than either. His long stride quickened to a
loping pace that soon brought him to a clearing where a
big Swede was frantically swinging a grubbing hoe to
deepen a trench around his cabin.

Sven turned up his sweat-streaked face as the
stranger crossed his clearing.

"You better run, man," Anders said. "It's coming
fast."

"No, by gar!" Sven shook his head. He wasn't
going to run off, letting his cabin go up in smoke.

But even as he spoke the black cloud, suffocating
and blinding, swept out of the woods; and fire was in
the air. Flames did not come over the ground, not yet;
but borne by that storm of heat and smoke, brands and
embers rained around him. In a quick blast the terrific
heat was there and all at once a blaze sprang up in the
top of a broken stump beside Sven's cabin. The next
moment the roof of the cabin was smoking. Now Anders
was shouting something, but his voice was lost in the
sudden roar of fire.

Sven looked once at the burning margin of his
clearing and then dived into his shanty to save what he
could. He came out with an empty water bucket, a
rifle, and the red petticoat that hung on his wall. Together he and Anders raced away.

The clearing was ablaze on three sides, and the only
way open was due south to the green timber, fortunately
too free from underbrush to hold the fire that dropped
from the wind. They ran till they could go no farther,
with the dense smoke choking in their throats and their

lungs near to bursting. They threw themselves flat on the ground, clawing out holes in the earth and thrusting their faces down to draw free air. They had no breath for words. When breath was in their bodies they found fires starting all about them. Sven managed one speech: "Tote road!" pointing with his rifle and looking surprised at the red petticoat in his hand. He dropped rifle, pail, and petticoat, and led the way to the tote road. There the smoke was almost blinding and the roaring pressed against their ears. Stopping to lie face down on the earth, they filled their lungs and ran on. During four hours they were not four feet apart and yet not a word passed between them. When they reached the sawdust streets of Peshtigo, the board sidewalks were already bursting into flame.

Fire was nothing new to Peshtigo. All through that dry summer the air had been full of smoke from brush fires on the railroad right of way. Occasionally those fires had spread and camp crews from the river or mill crews from the town had gone in to fight the blaze. People thought little of the pall of smoke that hung over the town and dulled the sun till it was like a red moon in the sky. But this was different. On this eighth day of October, 1871, a storm of wind swept through the woods with a leaping wall of fire. And Peshtigo lay dead in its path.

Panic-stricken, the people flocked out of smoke-filled houses into streets where the planking was on fire. They ran like sheep through the burning town, choking with smoke and shielding their faces from a heat that scorched men's beards. Scores, led by some insane impulse, crowded into the big boardinghouse below the mills.

They met fiery deaths when its walls collapsed like paper under the leaping blaze. Driven before the flames, hundreds of people plunged into the river. Some drowned promptly; others suffocated when the enormous rolls of smoke blew over. Many stood huddled together on the bridge. As the heat increased, maddened horses crowded onto the shaking span. Before the timbers could take fire, but not before the hair was burning on scores of human heads, the bridge collapsed. There was a general feeling that the world had come to an end, and dozens of people who might have been survivors committed suicide.

When the fire had burned itself out, sweeping over portions of four counties and leaving a dozen settlements in ashes, more than a thousand dead were counted. In Peshtigo, seven hundred people, half the town's population, were burned to death or died from burns or suffocation. With that incredible heat the marshland beyond the mills was baked to a depth of five feet. In Simmons's hardware store sixty dozen axes had run together in a single mass of hickory-studded iron; and the town fire engine was melted down where it stood in the ashes of the firemen's hall.

Swampers working up the Peshtigo and Oconto rivers didn't see a green tree all winter long, and they were as black as minstrels from handling the charred wood. In that country a tree but slightly burned would be worm-eaten within a year unless cut, and so the crews sledded the scarred trunks to the skidway and the mills. They found bodies of deer with the legs burned off and roasted carcasses of wolves and wildcats that had been trapped by the shifting flames. In the spring Sven Carl-

sten came back through the blackened woods to find his cabin. He shook his head and poked among the ashes. There was nothing left but a rusted coffeepot and a grubbing hoe with a charred handle. Not only ruin, but lonesomeness was to be his portion. Nowhere in the blackened forest did he find even a charred fragment of the red petticoat.

The logging methods of the prodigal years left cutover areas covered from five to forty feet deep with "slashings," dry as tinder. In a dry season these required but a spark from a passing locomotive, a sawmill, or a hunter's camp to start a blaze that might sweep the county. Within twenty years in the Wisconsin pineries there were the great fires of Peshtigo, Oshkosh, Phillips, Marshfield, Iron River, Fifield, and Medford.

As logging moved north, the great forest fires followed. In the nineties and the next decade it was Minnesota settlements, not Wisconsin towns, that saw the yellow glare in their autumn skies.

3

In the last week of August, 1894, gray skies too close and too clouded for heaven were moving over half the northern Minnesota counties. Day after day the sun circled the land like a dull-red coin, and night showed no stars in that still dark. Occasionally into Mission Creek, Sandstone, and Kettle River the wind brought a heavier fog that smarted in men's eyes and caught their throats. Whole counties, sharp with northern skies and the black and white of pines and aspens, had grown dim. After a gray and sudden dusk, with no faint line of color beyond the western forest, a scattered afterglow might play with a pale luminance, an afterglow that did not fade till the gray light rose upon the east. Boats moved at half speed on the rivers; trains crept with searchlights groping for the track; over Lake Superior the whalebacks passed in secret, and far away in the narrow rivers of the Soo they lay all night with engines idle, whistles crying in the dark.

In Pine County the smoke came down like night. For three days the Great Northern trains could not run. All this time the air was preternaturally still; the gray smother eddied in unfelt currents, settling on the rivers, blanketing the towns. People went vaguely to their work in a world devoid of landmarks; their eyes were sharp with the strangeness and uncertainty, their ears listened, even in sleep, for the clangor of church bells that would be their warning. They scoured the hooded skies and could read nothing there. Rain would be a mercy. "Brush fires," the warden said, twenty, thirty brush fires burning slowly, and countless peat fires eating the dry swamps in secret. Rain would be a mercy. Rain they dreamed of, tossing uneasily in close rooms at night, and in the morning their eyes went to the gray-blue blankness that pressed the windows.

Then at half past two on the afternoon of September 1st, a change was in the air. Far off there grew a sound, low at first, prolonged, rising. Hearts leapt and eyes pictured a heavier, darker sky and rain pelting the forest, rain coming like a wall across the north, rain and the cool damp smell of sodden woods. But the sound grew too quickly. The murmur rose to a roar and a wave of heat swept over. Then the full gale came, a sixty-mile gale, no gray pall now but white swirling smoke, and then it was fissured with a leaping color.

Instantly, in a storm, the fire struck Hinckley. Church bells rang a superfluous warning, and while the frightened sextons clung to the ropes the heated bells changed notes. At that the sextons ran terror-stricken to the streets. Ten minutes after the warning bells were started, every building in Hinckley was in flames.

On the railroad track a fireman frantically stoked the locomotive of a smoke-bound train. Engineer Jim Root pulled on the whistle cord, clamored with his high-pitched bell. Like a stampede the fear-crazed populace swept through burning streets. Three hundred of them climbed aboard as Jim Root got his driving rods into action. The engine coughed up black smoke, the big wheels spun on the rails. With his searchlight trailing the roadbed where the cedar ties were smoking, Jim Root backed his locomotive into the blazing forest. Before him fled the train of six coaches, four boxcars, and a caboose. At a curve the searchlight swept a pale finger over the receding town of flame. In that last glimpse of Hinckley, Jim Root saw figures racing through the streets. Grimly he held the throttle open.

The sky was black as midnight above the forest, but the track was walled in leaping light. Jim Root pushed his throttle wider. The fireman hurled coal through the open firebox door. His face was black as a hood with two burnt holes that showed his eyes. He was drenched in sweat; it kept his clothes from taking fire. But when he saw Jim Root's blue jacket smoking he dropped his shovel and doused him with water. By that time Jim Root had forgotten that his hand was blistering on the throttle; he was thinking of the dry bridge timbers over Grindstone Creek.

Grindstone Creek was a gulch of fire, but the bridge was there. An instant of lifting smoke showed deer circling blindly in the shallow stream. Then Jim Root saw something else—a glimpse of waving arms and lifted faces—before the smoke shut down again. By that time the ties were blazing under the wheels and fire broke out on the roofs of the wooden coaches. Jim Root held his throttle open. Before him, hurtling through smoke and fire, his heavy train thundered a mile a minute over burning bridges, through flame that spanned the railroad clearing. The fireman flung buckets of water through the cab to keep the flames from their clothing.

When the train, trailing the smoke of its own blazing cars, ground to a stop in Duluth with its three hundred and fifty survivors, Jim Root's bare hand was burned fast to the throttle. Behind them in the blackened forest lay the embers of six Minnesota towns, and somewhere in that waste were the burned bodies of four hundred and eighteen people who had missed the train.

CHAPTER 25

The Long Whistle

IN the late eighties the Clark House and the Hotel Spaulding in Duluth bustled with lumber barons from Michigan and Wisconsin—Mitchell and McClure, Merrill and Ring, Alger and Smith. The Mussers, Nortons, and Weyerhaeusers were moving from "downriver" into the North. For the "illimitable" tracts in the six great Wisconsin pineries were beginning to show a limit. Already the big firms had cruisers in every region of the Minnesota timber and soon sawmills were screaming night and day at Duluth-Superior, Cloquet, and Minneapolis.

Eastward, over the bright blue rim of Lake Superior, Minnesota lumber went to make everything from ship masts to matches.

Southward, in great rafts down the Mississippi, it went to build Omaha, Kansas City, Des Moines, St. Joseph, Wichita, Topeka, and big red barns on a thousand miles of prairie.

Rapidly the great lumber regions of Minnesota overshadowed the depleted pineries of Wisconsin. Now it was the Upper Mississippi, the St. Croix, St. Louis, Rum, Prairie, Swan, and Kettle rivers. North went the warning cry *Tim-mber-r-r!* and northward grew the thunder of the crashing pines. And northward to the woods swarmed Cleng Peerson's men. "Natural woodsmen," the Scandinavians filled the Minnesota camps, far outnumbering all other races. In the deep snow, over the frozen swamps, they swung their axes, rocked their saws, and drove their teams. And in the spring they thronged the Minnesota rivers, the most skillful and daring men who ever drove logs through white water.

In these years of America's expansion, "lumber" meant white pine, clear, straight, easy to work, fit for fifty building purposes. Nothing else was entered in the notes of cruisers. In that search for white pine, the lesser trees—cedar, hemlock, jack pine, poplar, tamarack —stood only in the way of logging sleds ready to load true lumber.

But soon the westward march of plow and railway brought a new demand, and cedar and tamarack came crying through the mills. With the land marked by fence lines from James River to the Arkansas, there was need for millions of cedar fence posts. Anton Poupoure came down to Lake Superior from Winnipeg and logged both sides of the St. Louis River, already stripped of pine, for cedar poles. Then Frederick Weyerhaeuser came up from the Wisconsin rivers and paid an even million dollars for the timber, land, and mills of the C. N. Nelson Lumber Company. Nelson was glad to get out, for he had sent every stick of pine down his driving streams, and people thought Fred Weyerhaeuser was crazy. But he made millions out of what Nelson had left behind—railroads bidding against each other for tamarack ties, paper mills clamoring for spruce, cedar posts and poles flowing like water through the mills, and the orders still growing. The Savannah River in one spring delivered a million railroad ties, besides great quantities of spruce, pulp, posts, poles, and saw logs. On the Nemadji River twenty-five million feet of logs were driven annually at the end of the century when thirty large sawmills were operating night and day in Duluth-Superior.

The end came quickly. In 1837 Franklin Steele and six half-breeds cut the first white pine in Minnesota. In 1912 there were forty thousand lumberjacks in the Minnesota forests. In 1926 the last great drive went down the historic St. Louis River, and John Cloudy landed six million feet of pine logs in the Whiteface River. That was the end. Now in all Duluth-Superior there is but one sawmill. In Minneapolis, Stillwater, Menomonie, Eau Claire, Virginia, the saws are quiet and the mills in ruin.

The vast enterprise lasted about a hundred years, from the first crude sawmills on the Wisconsin rivers in the 1820's till the long whistle sounded the end of operations in the timber ranges of Minnesota in the 1920's.

The long whistle wavering over the ruined forest was more than the symbol of the sawmill's end. It was the end of an empire, the brief and fabulous empire of logs. And when the echoes died away loneliness settled down. Grass grew up in the streets, the saloons and the dance halls decayed in the sun. Raspberry vines spread over the rusted rails of the logging line, the tote roads grew up in deer brush and aspen. The landing that had swarmed with teamsters, loaders, and whistle punks became a burrow for muskrats. The vast piratic enterprise left its empty camps and its abandoned towns scattered over the ruined North.

CHAPTER 26

Sawdust Town

THE Mississippi reaches its northernmost point
at Lake Bemidji in the Minnesota forests. From there
the dwindling stream, no larger than the Illinois creeks
which Cleng Peerson waded, curves southward toward
its headwaters at Itasca Lake. Remote and rugged, this
was one of the last wilderness regions of the Middle
Border. When the camps were abandoned on all the
lower tributaries, the logging men went farther north on
the Mississippi. The town of Bemidji became the center
of their operations, the last boom lumber town in all
the North.

Today a civic building stands beside the wind-
stirred waters of Lake Bemidji. There, along with other
civic properties, you may find a pile of newspapers, and
if you are curious the attendant will explain: "Old
newspaper file. First papers ever published in Bemidji."

On the wind comes the scream of the saws from
the Richardson mill, cutting up logs from a last stand
of Norway pine a few miles up the stripling Mississippi.

"And they *are* old," he adds emphatically—"eight-
een-ninety-eight."

He says it in all seriousness, and it is true. Time, as
we measure it in terms of change, began in these parts
north of the 47th parallel about 1895. Geographically
the first town on the Mississippi, Bemidji is chronolog-

ically the last settlement in all those miles between Lake Itasca and the Gulf of Mexico.

There are a hundred towns and cities that the Father of Waters has nourished, and to name any half dozen of them over—Minneapolis, La Crosse, Keokuk, Galena, Rock Island, Hannibal—is a certain American music and evokes in unexpected ways the American story.

None is more evocative than Bemidji. Because it was a frontier settlement it attracted a variety of folk to the whole north region. A twenty-mile circle drawn around Bemidji includes the towns of Naytahwaush, Fernhill, Gunder, Ebro, Laporte—five nations and five languages in one corner of a county. In Bemidji are names from all the latest immigrations, Finnish and Icelandic, German, Polish, and Scandinavian, as well as the Scotch and Irish names that have followed the logging roads from Maine to Oregon. Beside them are the old and new Ojibway names, Nashawauk and Kitichi, Jim Rollingstone and John Otherday, and the commonplace pair, Joe Salt and Joe Pepper. Add Paul Hollandaise and Pierre Ciel, the French Canadians still retaining their instinct for the forest, unchanged since the wilderness first made them over with the canoe, the sheath knife, and the buckskin jacket three hundred years ago. With the names go the dozen dialects to be heard in the street, from the muttered uneasy music of Ojibway to the singsong syllables of Scandinavian. It is inevitable that the folk stories of the North are dialect stories: The Swede driver says at the end of a trip into the back country, "Vell, mister, Ae jusually get two dawlers for dis har trip, but on account bad vedder an' rough roads do ju tenk dawler en half ban too mutts?" The old Finn watchman at the railroad track says, "Now you no tell-a me what I tol-a you," and he means, "Don't tell anybody." The French Canadian says, "You know, t'e cran-berr'. You put him on t'e stove in a leetle water an' cook him op, an' by gar, he make more better applesauce t'an t'e prune!"

More even than most middle western towns, Bemidji has known the quick change and sudden seasons of American enterprise. Tamarack grew in its streets in 1895. The first settlers came over the swamped-out trails, their whiffletrees banging against the stumps in the road. In those days the pinery seemed limitless and inexhaustible. But in twenty years it was gone. The saw-mill camp springing up in a season, the railroad coming and the place a boom town, with log trains on the way day and night, and the slash piling up faster than fire could burn it, the millionaires arriving, the mills expanding, and then the end of riches and a land laid waste—this is a familiar sequence in America. Elsewhere the forest might have been cut in terms of conservation and the mills might have run for centuries, but the lumber barons did business in another way. By bribing and scheming, by lobbying and lawyering and downright thievery, they got possession of the pinelands. "Why, them buzzards, they could steal a log out of the bark with a man a-straddle of it." Stolen logs cut as many board feet as any other. But in twenty years it was over. Now one sawmill is left operating in Bemidji, and Minnesota imports lumber every year from Russia, Finland, and Estonia.

Bemidji has come of age. The old Remore Hotel, with the pike poles crossed above its door, is gone; where the lumber barons gathered and the calked boots of swampers clattered by, now a "lubrication center" dispenses three grades of gasoline and a line of tires from Akron, Ohio. The lake shore, once scarred with logs and pitted with the thrusts of peaveys, is parked and gardened. A Carnegie library replaces a sawmill on the bay. But with a certain nostalgia for sawdust the Bemidji *Daily Pioneer* prints a reminiscent column, "Thirty Years Ago."

The flavor is not gone. On the terraced lake front stands a nine-foot figure of the great Chippewa chief, Bemidji, carved from a pine log by an unknown lumberjack. It is a naïve figure, almost womanly with the black hair streaming down the shoulders and a hand raised to shield the peering eyes. Yet someway it manages to resemble the storied chief—his face like that of a great and noble dog, voiceless, tragic, and enduring. With a curious clairvoyance the big chief peers across the lake to a sawmill's smoking chimney; it was lumber that dispossessed the Chippewas. If you walk along the river, the Mississippi that is like a trout stream in these forests of balsam and Norway pine, you see the stray logs that escaped the last spring drives when the men broke the jams and kept the great tide moving on the April stage of water. Now, along Jim Hill's railroad the ground has a peculiar yielding, a soft, elastic dust, and you remember that Bemidji had fourteen sawmills and cut a million feet of lumber every day—the band saws screaming at noon and midnight, the forty-two blades of the gang saw turning pine logs into building lumber.

Scratch Bemidji and you find sawdust. Look under the bridges and you see the old landing logs from the camps. People still sleep on mattresses of sawdust and shavings, and in back yards the boys chop kindling with the swamper's double-bladed ax. And you can still see men here who entered the country with ox teams, who poled rafts up the rivers and ran logs down them. They have memories that seem farther than a lifetime away from the WPA projects and the CCC camps that dot the second growth of Beltrami and Itasca counties.

The paradox of a WPA project for compiling the history of a frontier community is only one more evidence of the ironic changes which have come over American life in the past half-century. These changes account for the sag in some of the faces and the strained listlessness that may be felt in the circle of men at night on a street corner of Bemidji. It is the familiar story of frontier energies left without object after the pioneer life has passed. The frontier gave men certain idioms and these have maintained themselves, often finding their way into our common language and enriching it. It also gave them certain qualities, skills, abilities, and attitudes. And these have lasted longer than the conditions which produced them. The memory lingers sometimes ironically. So it is that the crossroads filling station, with its side line of soft drinks and chocolate bars, still is labeled "Trading Post"! The irony is more pointed when a man finds no use for the abilities his life has taught him. Take the old telegraph operator, Grant Bramble, who learned to use a pistol when there were few arts or sciences so important; now he sits all day in the little Chicago &

North-Western station at Sleepy Eye and shoots flies on the ceiling. And he never misses.

The mouth of the Mississippi was known two hundred years before its source. The French flag flew above the compound at New Orleans, and then the Spanish, and the French again, while the Sioux and the Chippewas waged their long warfare in the forest. Yet the upper river drew men after it. So, in time expeditions came to chart its headwaters. They followed it north until it turned upon itself, and then they were bewildered, seeing that the great southward sweeping river begins its flow toward Hudson Bay. At last, though it was many years and half a dozen explorations before they set their transits there, they stood at the north end of Lake Itasca and saw the river born.

They found the river's beginning, but not for a hundred years did history come after them. Only when America felt the pull of destiny in the West, when Jim Hill and Jay Cooke and Leland Stanford pushed their steel paths across the continent, was there a force great enough to possess the wilderness out of which America's river came. Then the sound of axes drifted up the great valley, from La Crosse to Reads Landing, from Beef Slough to Little Falls. The camps spread northward; down the river went the great log rafts. Eight hundred rafts of pine passed Burlington in a single season. So the sun struck through to the trampled ferns and the log-scarred earth along the rivers; and Wisconsin pine grew into Kansas cities, while the sawmill screamed where the loon had been. History had come to the last wilderness.

In this sense the first copies of the Bemidji newspaper seem old. They are as old as the difference between oxcarts on the tote roads and streamlined traffic on U. S. 2. Their story is as American as all stories of man's beginning in a wilderness, and it goes as deeply into the past as John Smith's landing on Virginia shores or the anchoring of a vessel named *Mayflower* in Massachusetts Bay.

PART FOUR

The River Today

CHAPTER 27

From St. Louis to St. Paul

A CENTURY ago the "western fever" brought the Mississippi its hectic, fervid life, and when the fever passed the languid river was lined with useless warehouses and weed-grown landings. A lifetime was enough to span the rise of the trade and its decline, and there were many rivermen who knew Mark Twain's sense of loss when the great arched bridges carried a land-borne commerce on its way with hardly a glance at the empty current below. The river commerce began in 1820. It reached its height in thirty years, and another thirty years brought the end. The railroads banished the steamboats from the landings, as they had driven the stage coach and the covered wagon from the prairie trails. Fifty years ago the Mississippi seemed relegated to history, and a fading folklore. It had served its time. But the vast current still moved on to the sea.

The rediscovery of the river came in 1917. With the demands of war the railroads were hopelessly overwhelmed. Millions of tons of vital materials accumulated at the terminals, waiting to be moved to tidewater. In a desperate effort to break that jam of war goods the government took over all available craft on the western rivers. Using steamboats and barges, linking warehouses and terminals, merging local carriers into a hasty system of long-distance transport, the Federal Barge Lines were established. Despite enormous problems and difficulties, they moved the goods.

The necessity of war had discovered a forgotten resource in mid-America. The rivers were a highway, cheap, efficient, capable of carrying a prodigious tonnage. When the war was over there was a new demand for cheap transportation in the Middle West. With the war experience fresh in their minds midwestern congressmen framed the Transportation Act of 1920, an act which maintained the government in business on the rivers, not only operating its own barge lines but beginning a far-reaching program of channel improvement and terminal construction. In 1924 the barge lines were made the basis of an enlarged federal organization, the Inland Waterways Corporation, which began operations with nearly two hundred towboats and barges. Its purpose was to open the way for private enterprise on the rivers and it proposed to sell out its facilities as soon as private business was ready to take over.

The commerce grew and the purpose became realized. In 1920 there was an annual movement of twenty-five million tons on the Mississippi system. Twenty years later the commerce had reached an annual volume of more than a hundred million tons, of which the federal lines carried only three per cent.

The first operations were located on the Ohio and Lower Mississippi rivers, and it was not until 1928 that the barge lines began a pioneer service on the Upper Mississippi. Using light barges of five hundred tons' capacity they sent their towboats up the river from St. Louis. Slowly, cautiously, poking their way into channels that had not carried cargo for forty years, they made their passage up the river. They proved what could be done. Then the army engineers began work on a system of locks and dams which would open the Upper Mississippi to an important volume of trade. Their design was to make the river between St. Louis and St. Paul into a long series of navigable pools, governed by dams, with an unvarying nine-foot channel. It was an enormous task, parts of which could not be realized for many years. But in 1937 the initial program was complete, and . to celebrate the undertaking the veteran steamboat *Golden Eagle* embarked on a triumphant voyage up the river.

The voyage of the *Golden Eagle* was a rediscovery of the Upper Mississippi and it provided an event almost as epoch-making as the voyage of the tiny stern-wheeler *Virginia* a hundred and fourteen years before. All the way to St. Paul crowds lined the river front and the new lock walls—not Indians and trappers this time, but midwestern businessmen, farmers, and townspeople with their automobiles parked in long rows on the landings. They cheered and sang and shouted as the steamboat churned past. Aboard the *Golden Eagle* sounded the steady thump of the engines and the creak of the steering gear. Many times there were bated breaths in the pilothouse and strained faces in the engine room. Aboard the steamer and ashore rivermen were shaking their heads, saying the *Golden Eagle* would never get through. But she did. The Upper Mississippi was navigated again, triumphantly, through a series of new channels and past a system of enormous dikes and dams. A new era had come to the river.

Like the historic *Virginia*, the *Golden Eagle* made

her way up an empty river, breasting the current, slipping between the islands, skirting the bars. But it was a different country she passed through. What the *Virginia* saw was land merely, no land in particular. The *Golden Eagle* saw a country shaped and colored by a century of experience, a region marked by men and events, a land with character and history.

All the way it was a revealing voyage, eloquent with things that change and with things that are changeless, crowded with memories and with prospects. The *Virginia* had steamed away from St. Louis when Dube's ferry still did service across the Mississippi. That ferry was a pirogue—two square-sterned log canoes lashed together with poles and floored over with rough planking. It was rigged with a mast and a flapping square sail, but there was always work for two oarsmen, one at the bow and another beside a steering oar at the stern. In those days many pirogues came to St. Louis from the Missouri, carrying bear's fat, or occasionally wild honey, in a middle compartment of the dugout shell. It was a profitable trade. Hogs were scarce and lard was high; bear's fat was a cheap and useful substitute. So the pirogue was the river's first tanker—where today the oil barges float their 8,500 barrels' capacity.

Where the *Virginia* churned across the path of Dube's ferry, the *Golden Eagle* steamed under the great arch of the Eads Bridge. The bridge is a monument to Captain James B. Eads who more than eighty years ago proposed to an indifferent Congress a program for improving and maintaining the river channels. Now time has come round to him. He saw St. Louis, rising on its broad terraces above the river, as the great commercial depot of the Mississippi valley, and events have proved him right. Today, with a greater commerce on the river than ever in the past, the city which grew from Pierre Laclede's trading post is the capital of the Inland Waterways.

Some of the river towns have not found the greatness they dreamed of. Louisiana, Missouri, was founded in the years when Timothy Flint looked at the lawless territories beyond the river and said, "When we cross the Mississippi we travel beyond the Sabbath." The village of Louisiana plotted its future on paper and breathed the heady air of expectation. But the expansion passed it by and now it is a drowsy place famed chiefly as the home of the legendary Jim Bludso, engineer of the *Prairie Belle,* whom John Hay gave a lasting life in his Pike County Ballads.

> Wall, no! I can't tell whar he lives,
>   Because he don't live, you see;
> Leastways, he's got out of the habit
>   Of livin' like you and me.
> What have you been for the last three year
>   That you haven't heard folks tell
> How Jimmy Bludo passed in his checks,
>   The night of the Prairie Belle?
>
> He weren't no saint,—them engineers
>   Is all pretty much alike,—
> One wife in Natchez-under-the-Hill
>   And another one here, in Pike;
> A keerless man in his talk, was Jim,
>   And an awkward man in a row,
> But he never flunked, and he never lied,—
>   I reckon he never knowed how.

And this was all the religion he had,—
  To treat his engine well;
Never be passed on the river;
  To mind the pilot's bell;
And if ever the Prairie Belle took fire,—
  A thousand times he swore
He'd hold her nozzle agin the bank
  Till the last soul got ashore.

All boats has their day on the Mississip,
  And her day come at last,—
The Movastar was a better boat,
  But the Belle she *wouldn't* be passed.
And so she come tearin' along through the night—
  The oldest craft on the line—
With a nigger squat on her safety-valve,
  And her furnace crammed, rosin and pine.

The fire bust out as she clared the bar,
  And burnt a hole in the night,
And quick as a flash she turned, and made
  For that willer-bank on the right.
There was runnin' and cursin', but Jim yelled out,
  Over all the infernal roar,
"I'll hold her nozzle agin the bank
  Till the last galoot's ashore."

Through the hot, black breath of the burnin' boat
  Jim Bludso's voice was heard,
And they all had trust in his cussedness,
  And knowed he would keep his word.
And, sure's you're born, they all got off
  Afore the smoke-stacks fell,—
And Bludso's ghost went up alone
  In the smoke of the Prairie Belle.

He weren't no saint—but at jedgment
　　I'd run my chance with Jim,
Longside of some pious gentlemen
　　That wouldn't shook hands with him.
He seen his duty, a dead-sure thing—
　　And went for it thar and then!
And Christ ain't a goin' to be too hard
　　On a man that died for men.

The past lingers on in Louisiana and now a visitor can see the very willow where Jim held his boat against the bank while he scalded to death at his engines' throttles.

Hannibal and Quincy have grown to bustling towns, and Keokuk, still bearing the name of a Sauk chief, rises above its great new dam. Burlington surveys the river from a gracious height, looking down the valley where the Mormons once fled from the wrath of their gentile neighbors. Above the entrance of the Iowa River, the Mississippi is framed by the busy industrial life of the Tri-Cities—Moline and Rock Island on the Illinois side and Davenport spreading handsomely on the hills of Iowa. Their future is brightened by the new commerce on the river, a commerce that will bring increasing quantities of oil and ore and carry away the plows and grain of their factories and elevators. Clinton and Dubuque have long river histories, and La Crosse was once a famous lumber port. Now their sky lines have spread and changed, but the river front still harbors the old warehouses, the fish docks, and the shanty boats. Soon new terminals will come to handle the freight trade that is growing year by year.

Above La Crosse the river is the center of an extensive area of the National Wild Life Refuge. For scores of miles the Winnesheik Bottoms present a network of sloughs and bayous, a natural fish hatchery and breeding ground, and a feeding ground for millions of wild fowl which every spring and fall travel the great Mississippi flyway. Now the federal government controls a vast area, 175,000 acres of land and 100,000 acres of water surface, as a national game preserve. Here is the completed cycle. Where river travelers a century ago heard tales of giant catfish, big enough to overturn a canoe, and saw flocks of wild fowl that shadowed the sky, now men are at work to protect the fish and game that a few years ago were threatened with extinction.

It is still a beautiful river, winding at the base of limestone bluffs, mirroring the feathery foliage of willow banks and the dark contours of forest-patterned slopes. At the foot of Lake Pepin is the village of Reads —once Reads Landing and famous for its burly life of lumberjacks, raftsmen, immigrants, and speculators. Now only a weathered row of mooring spiles remains to mark the vanished traffic, the miles of pine logs in the river, and the long lines of grain wagons bringing wheat to the steamboat landing.

As the Mississippi nears St. Paul the gorge narrows and deepens. To Peter Pond and Jonathan Carver, to Zebulon Pike and Henry Schoolcraft it was an impressive sight, and time has not changed it in that regard; it remains one of the most beautiful stretches among all of America's rivers. At its upper end the gorge is framed by the sky lines of the Twin Cities. Since the *Virginia's* arrival, Pig's Eye, named for the infamous one-eyed trader, Pierre Parrant, has become the capital city and commercial metropolis of St. Paul, and the saw-mill town of St. Anthony has become the spacious, gracious city of Minneapolis, combining in its name the native and the classical, the Sioux word for water and the Greek word for city. In 1860 a single flour mill in Minneapolis sent occasional cargoes down the river. Now the mills line the river like palisades and St. Anthony's Falls are nearly obliterated by dams and diversions.

The *Virginia* arrived under the walls of Fort Snelling, with the Indians staring and the wilderness dark around. The *Golden Eagle* came to a triumphant berth under the sky line of St. Paul. It is the same river, but a civilization had taken shape between the two voyages.

Though the voyage of the *Golden Eagle* was a picturesque event, it did not really represent the new era on the river. The twentieth century commerce is a movement not of steamers but of barges, not of passengers but of freight. The splendor of the steamboats is replaced by a plodding business in grain and gravel, oil and fertilizer, steel and stone. There are no races down the river, no music and dancing, no crowds waiting at the levees. But it is a vastly more important commerce than was carried by the fleets that once lined the river front at St. Louis and St. Paul.

At the height of the steamboat age in the 1850's the annual volume of goods carried on the western rivers was ten million tons. Today the barge lines transport more than ten times that tonage of bulk and packaged freight. Only a fraction of this total is borne on the Upper Mississippi, but still it is a bigger tonnage than the steamboats ever carried on the upper river, and it is growing by a million tons each year. From St. Paul and Minneapolis and the terminal towns in Illinois and Iowa go great quantities of flour and grain, steel plows and threshing machines, soybeans and lumber. Up the river come ponderous cargoes of oil and sulphur, sugar and scrap iron, coffee, rice, and fertilizer. Now the streamliners race northward along the river and streak across the arched bridges to the west, but the barge fleets, plodding in the current, are the freight trains of the valley.

They are many freight trains, made up, like an assortment of boxcars and tank cars, flatcars and gondolas, of carriers adapted to their cargo. In a single tow there are open barges, covered barges, tank barges, hopper barges. Each barge has a capacity of from five hundred to fifteen hundred tons, which makes it equivalent to an entire freight train, and a single tow of ten barges often carries a cargo in excess of ten thousand tons. Tows of this size equal the capacity of large ocean freighters, and they dwarf the romantic packet boats that have vanished from the river. They give the railroads a bad case of nerves, because one towboat can push a string of barges equal in tonnage to five or six long freight trains and can move bulk goods at about half the railroad rate.

Of course it is a slow way to market. Top speed for a tow is six miles an hour, and to make that a tow must be going downstream in a good current. The average rate for tows moving upstream is three miles an hour. A towboat captain must be a patient man, willing to get there tomorrow if he can't make it today. There are

scores of locks to pass, each one requiring time and patience, and there are stretches of swift current where the tow must be "divided." This is a long, exacting job, casting off half the barges, taking one part through to quiet water, securing it there and going back for the other part, finally merging the two together again. So a "tow" voyage takes weeks, as it did for the flatboats and the keelboats before the age of steam. But it delivers mountains of cargo.

Towboats, the locomotives of the river traffic, are without exception "push boats." With their vast loads ahead of them they labor through the current. Pushing gives the wheelsmen a clear view of his load, which may be several times as big as a football field, and also of the river. Besides, the tow is easier to handle when it is pushed and a boat has more pushing than pulling power. The new towboats are powered with twin Diesel engines and are thoroughly equipped for the comfort of the crew and the safety of the cargo. Two-way radio systems keep them constantly in touch with the main dispatching office, and a loud-speaker carries orders from the pilothouse to the front of the tow, which may be a quarter of a mile away.

This large-scale commerce has been made possible by a vast system of river improvements and aids to navigation. Government engineers have regulated channels, putting in cuts, dikes, and dams, and have given the river a uniformity and permanence which nature would never provide. Their task goes on endlessly, for even with those vast restraints the river is not tamed. Survey boats thrash through the current on their ceaseless mission, sounding the channel, changing markers, checking the ranges and the lights. River shoals are always shifting —a bar may move a mile within a month—and so the channels must be freshly marked and the bends accurately lighted.

River lights are uniformly white, set on heavy posts twelve feet high and equipped with props, crossarms, a stairway, and a lamp bracket. The brass lamp burns mineral oil, night and day, and must be refilled every seventy-two hours. As there are some eight hundred lights between St. Louis and St. Paul, the tending of them is a business in itself. No survey boat, or fleet of boats, could make the rounds of all those lights. They are locally manned, in charge of men, and occasionally women, who live along the river. For a payment of ten dollars a light they keep the flame burning, move it to safety in case of flood, set up emergency beacons if the river should abandon its channel. The lanterns are nearly windproof and will burn in a gale of great violence. But despite high winds and high water, November snowstorms and April fogs, the fuel must be replenished and the flame kept burning at the water's edge. The lightkeepers have created a tradition of faithful, devoted, and often heroic service.

The big efficient business of the barge lines, the channel improvements, the radio systems, and the aids to navigation have not done away with the craft of piloting on the river. The old-time steamboatmen had to "read the waters" for bars and shoals, to listen for a dog's bark on a foggy night or to judge the shore by the whistle's echo rolling along the bluffs. They had to take their boats through rapid water and to squeeze through tight places. Those arts have not changed or lessened.

The towboatman must know the river in daylight and in darkness. He must know every shore light and every channel marker; he must remember sand bars, crossings, cutoffs, bends, sloughs, and bridges. From the distant bow of the forward barges the watchman calls the soundings, *Mar-r-r-k Three, Quarter-less-Three* . . . *Half-Twain* . . . *Quarter-Twain* . . . *Mar-r-r-k Twain*, and in the pilothouse the big spokes turn over. It is the old voice on the river, and the old tradition.

CHAPTER 28

Another Harvest

THE Upper Mississippi valley has bred many men who helped to shape the life of America. Some, like U. S. Grant, fought its wars, some, like Mark Twain, wrote its books, some, like Ignatius Donnelly, dreamed its unfulfilled dreams. One of them helped to interpret America to itself and to the world. He offered a conception of American civilization which the social experience of the great valley illustrated most completely and dramatically. By seeing the development of democracy in the hazards and hardships, the ventures and aspirations of the frontier, he has contributed deeply to the understanding of America.

Frederick Jackson Turner grew up in the town of Portage, Wisconsin, where voyageurs, priests, and traders once carried their canoes from the Fox River to the Wisconsin, bound from the Great Lakes to the Mississippi. From his boyhood, he wondered about his country. He knew Portage and its people; he was familiar with the mixed speech of settlers, the Germans, the Yankees, and the big, gentle-voiced Scandinavians. He knew men who had broken the prairie sod and planted their first crops in wild earth; and on the streets of Portage he saw men who walked with the tentative step of the forest, not depending on a straight road and a graded way but by habit and rhythm walkers over blowdowns and around tree stumps and the granite that the glacier had strewn beside the rivers. He thought of the rich produce that land had made in furs, minerals, timber, grain, cattle; and he saw deeper than that to another harvest, the contribution of men who possessed imagination and will, a common strain among the several races. He saw men drawing from the frontier, that was their memory and tradition, a certain nurture; though the age was past, their minds kept its rhythms and knew its vitality.

Himself a man like these, Frederick Jackson Turner undertook a lifelong study of the national history. He brought to his task a mind that constantly searched for new viewpoints and foundations. He interpreted American development in terms of geography, geology, economics, as well as political institutions. Indeed, he made it clear that institutions were a product of the social life, which in turn was colored by the physical, racial, and psychological aspects of sections. He saw older American institutions moving across the continent with the migrant folk, but undergoing subtle and far-reaching changes as they served the needs of people in new surroundings: the frontier, acting with mighty power upon the minds and manners of men, forced them to active democracy, shaping their organization to their needs. He saw that the whole history of man in his emergence from brutality and his slow, truceless encounter with nature was repeated in a single generation on the Middle Border, and so he saw that America had a history unlike any other in the world. He devoted his life to considering that profound American drama—people with six thousand years of civilized tradition subjecting themselves and their society to the naked power of wind, earth, and water, and finding their life tested, stripped of false implements, altered and strengthened by it. Thus was conceived the most original and significant approach to the problems of American national development.

A short compact figure, who never lost the youthful spring in his stride and the light in his blue eyes, Frederick Jackson Turner was a man pursuing America's meanings as his Connecticut forbears had sought new lands in the West. Late in life he sat beside the Pacific at Carmel and wrote, "This is a beautiful place to sit and consider America." But to Turner all places were beautiful places for considering America, and none more so than Portage, the Wisconsin town of his boyhood; a boyhood close to the streams and forests, lighted with the color of a wilderness not yet gone and a people who still retained the rude and easy ways of new country. Later, learning frontier politics in the office of the village paper, he saw the pioneer life evolving its organs of political existence.

He never forgot his early youth, and in his years of study his mind went back to those rivers, one flowing toward the St. Lawrence, the other to the Gulf of Mexico, to renew his sense of the forces by which the national life was nurtured. He could call back the immigrant boats on the Mississippi, the men in homespun, the women with babies in their arms, and the sound of a dozen tongues in those Wisconsin counties. And he could envisage the process in a thousand towns and villages, settlers becoming citizens, with the powerful forces of the wilderness determining their minds and their bonds with each other.

So the land shaped the people, and in time the people shaped the land. And despite the changes of history the land still keeps its elemental rhythms. From their wilderness camp in 1659, Radisson and Groseilliers passed over the frozen swamps and lifeless rivers of a country starkly beautiful, locked in cold. But suddenly, in April, the land came to life, all its rivers flowing white and loud. Overnight the forest held the sound of runing water; every valley kept a thread of light. With careful hands the voyageurs traced the rivers on their contour maps; all at once their maps were living.

Since then time has brought many changes, but not this. Over all the map of America spread the rivers, like the lines in a man's hand. And in the Middle Border the same lines are there that the coureurs de bois marked down three centuries ago, the fine lines growing strong as they draw toward the Mississippi.

The northern spring comes quickly and with beauty. Beside the little streams that become the Mississippi, the dark earth emerges from the snow. The small flowers, blue and golden, star the wet earth at the edge of snowbanks. After the long silence, wind and water, the oldest sounds in the world, resume again; and the water runs in tune to man's blood, bringing back life to the land.

SELECTED BIBLIOGRAPHY

Books

BLAIR, WALTER, *A Raft Pilot's Log*. Cleveland, 1930.

BLEGEN, THEODORE C. (trans.), *Ole Rynning's True Account of America*. Minneapolis, 1926.

Burton Historical Collection Leaflet, Vols. 1-10. Detroit, 1922-1931.

CARVER, JONATHAN, *Travels through the Interior Parts of North America in the Years 1766, 1767, and 1768*. New York, 1838.

DAYTON, FRED E., and ADAMS, JOHN W., *Steamboating Days*. New York, 1925.

FLINT, TIMOTHY, *Recollections of the Last Ten Years*. Cincinnati, 1826.

FOLWELL, WILLIAM WATTS, *A History of Minnesota* (4 vols.). St. Paul, 1922.

GLAZIER, CAPTAIN WILLARD, *Down the Great River*. Philadelphia, 1889.

HALL, JAMES, *Sketches of History, Life and Manners in the West*. Cincinnati, 1834.

HARTSOUGH, MILDRED, *From Canoe to Steel Barge on the Upper Mississippi*. Minneapolis, 1934.

KELLOGG, LOUISE PHELPS, *The French Régime in Wisconsin and the Northwest*. Madison, 1925.

LINN, WILLSON ALEXANDER, *The Story of the Mormons*. New York, 1902.

MARK TWAIN'S AUTOBIOGRAPHY. New York, 1924.

MERRICK, GEORGE BYRON, *Old Times on the Upper Mississippi*. Cleveland, 1910.

Minnesota: A State Guide. New York, 1938.

Missouri: A Guide to the Show Me State. New York, 1941.

OGG, FREDERICK AUSTIN, *The Opening of the Mississippi*. New York, 1904.

PAINE, ALBERT BIGELOW, *Mark Twain: A Biography*. New York, 1912.

PETERSEN, WILLIAM J., *Steamboating on the Upper Mississippi*. Iowa City, 1937.

PUTNAM, GEORGE R., *Lighthouses and Lightships of the United States*. Boston, 1923.

QUICK, HERBERT AND EDWARD, *Mississippi Steamboatin'*. New York, 1926.

SCHARF, J. THOMAS, *History of St. Louis County and City* (2 vols.). Philadelphia, 1883.

SCHOOLCRAFT, HENRY ROWE, *Narrative of an Expedition through the Upper Mississippi to Itasca Lake*. New York, 1834.

THWAITES, REUBEN GOLD (ed.), *Wisconsin Historical Collections*.

TOUSLEY, ALBERT S., *Where Goes the River*. Iowa City, 1928.

Wisconsin: A Guide to the Badger State. New York, 1941.

PERIODICALS

American Historical Review
Iowa Journal of History and Politics
Minnesota History
Mississippi Valley Historical Review
Missouri Historical Review
Wisconsin History

Index